A Second Book of 75 Secondary Assembly Notes

(Including Senior Student Assemblies)

by Lawrie Baker, B.A.
(Former Head of Villiers High School, Southall)

W. FOULSHAM & CO. LIMITED
Yeovil Road, Slough, Berks., England

Foreword

Those responsible for taking assemblies find, inevitably, that they need to draw on a variety of source material to meet the continuing demands of school collective worship.

It is gratifying to learn that the first book of **75 Secondary Assembly Notes** has helped to fulfil this need. It has been an encouragement to publish a second book following the same format. Each assembly has a framework with a theme and a set of notes in logical sequence, within which those taking the assemblies can express their own personality and ideas. As before, there is a space provided at the end of each assembly for leaders to make their own notes.

The Sixth Form Assemblies of the previous book are replaced by Senior Student Assemblies which are intended to cover Years 10, 11 and 12, but can be used, at the leader's discretion, for other years.

Acknowledgements

Despite every effort it has not been possible to trace the source of all the material.
If an author's copyright has been infringed, sincere regrets are tendered.

The Publishers are grateful for permission to use the follwing in this collection:

Manchester City Art Gallery for 'The Shadow of the Cross' by William Holman Hunt.

Extracts from 'Poems for the Fallen' reproduced by permission of Mrs. Nicolette Grey and The Society of Authors, on behalf of the Laurence Binyon Estate.

Amnesty International, 99–119 Roseberry Avenue, London EC1R 4RE for 'A litany for the Day of Human Rights' by Salvador de Madiariaga

'The Lord of the Dance' by Sydney Carter reproduced by permission of Stainer & Bell Ltd., London, England.

John Murray (Publishers) Ltd. for the poem Christmas from 'The Collected Poems of John Betjeman'.

'Somewhere in this....' reproduced from 'Oceans of Prayer' compiled by Maureen Edwards and Jan S Pickard with the permission of the National Christian Education Council.

All Rights Reserved. No part of this publication may be
reproduced, stored in a retrieval system, or transmitted in any
form or by any means, electronic, mechanical, photocopying,
recording or otherwise, without the prior permission of the
Copyright owner.

ISBN 0-572-01993-9
Copyright © Lawrie Baker 1994
Printed and bound in Great Britain at The Bath Press, Avon

CONTENTS

General Assemblies

Page No.

- 4 Christmas
- 5 Hospitals
- 6 Sikhism – Guru Tegh Bahadur
- 7 Parents
- 9 Pets
- 10 Home
- 11 Reliability
- 12 Giving
- 14 The Tongue
- 15 Remembrance Day
- 17 End of Term
- 18 Sikhism
- 20 World Problems
- 22 Islam
- 23 End of School Year
- 25 Leavers' Assembly
- 26 Selflessness
- 28 Work
- 29 Christmas Decorations and Preparations
- 31 Maundy Thursday
- 33 Good Friday and Easter Sunday
- 35 Whitsun
- 36 Peacemaking – Archbishop Desmond Tutu
- 38 Offering Help and Advice
- 39 Hinduism – Holi
- 40 Hunger
- 41 Three Chinese Festivals
- 43 Honesty
- 44 Being Thankful

Page No.

- 46 Water
- 48 Spring
- 49 Sword of Damocles
- 50 Mothering Sunday
- 52 Concentration
- 54 National Children's Home
- 55 Town Planning
- 57 Haves and Havenots
- 59 Blindness
- 61 Writing on the Wall
- 63 Talents
- 64 Community Responsibility
- 66 April
- 67 Amnesty International
- 69 Peace-Keeping
- 71 Dancing
- 73 Attention to Detail
- 75 Sincerity
- 76 Patience
- 77 Harvest of the Sea
- 79 Death of Member of School

Senior Student Assemblies

Page No.

- 82 Morality
- 83 Determination
- 85 Friendship
- 88 Vanity, Vanity
- 90 The Environment

Page No.

- 91 Violence
- 93 Age of Television
- 94 Christmas
- 97 Mind over Matter
- 98 Ageism
- 100 Science and Religion
- 102 Pesach – Jewish Passover
- 104 Nationalism
- 106 Euthanasia
- 107 In the Beginning
- 110 Slavery
- 112 Murder
- 113 Religions
- 115 Poverty
- 116 Refugees
- 118 Handel's Messiah – Christmas
- 119 Shintoism
- 120 Holy Week Art and Religion
- 122 The Future – What Does it Hold?
- 124 Despair
- 127 Holman Hunt's "The Shadow of The Cross"
- 128 Index

CHRISTMAS

1   Christmas comes in winter – dark nights, often bad weather.

   Time for cheering ourselves up, for enjoyment.

2   Meant to be time for celebrating Christ's birth.

   (Though exact date of Christ's birth uncertain, has been celebrated on 25th December in West since 336AD)

3   Hopefully time for showing kindness, care, goodwill.

4   For some, however, glad tidings of Christmas mean nothing.

   Charles Dickens wrote story of such a man, Scrooge, in *A Christmas Carol*.
   Here is part of the conversation between Scrooge and his nephew:
   'A Merry Christmas, Uncle! God save you!' cried a cheerful voice. It was the voice of Scrooge's nephew…
   'Bah!' said Scrooge. 'Humbug!'…
   'Christmas a humbug, Uncle!' said Scrooge's nephew. 'You don't mean that, I'm sure?'
   'I do' said Scrooge. 'Merry Christmas! What right have you to be merry? You're poor enough.'
   'Come then,' returned the nephew gaily 'What right have you to be dismal? What reason have you to be morose? You're rich enough!'
   Scrooge, having no better answer ready on the spur of the moment, said. 'Bah!' again, and followed it up with 'Humbug!'… 'Keep Christmas in your own way, and let me keep it in mine!'
   'Keep it!' repeated Scrooge's nephew. 'But you don't keep it.'
   'Let me leave it alone, then,' said Scrooge. 'Much good may it do you! Much good it has ever done you!'
   'There are many things from which I might have derived good by which I have not profited, I dare say,' returned the nephew, 'Christmas among the rest. But I'm sure I have always thought of Christmas time, when it has come round – apart from the veneration due to its sacred name and origin, if anything belonging to it can be apart from that – as a good time; a kind, forgiving, charitable, pleasant time; the only time I know of, in the long calendar of the year, when men and women seem by one consent to open their shut-up hearts freely, and to think of people below them as if they really were fellow passengers to the grave, and not another race of creatures bound on other journeys. And therefore, Uncle, though it has never put a scrap of gold or silver in my pocket, I believe that it *has* done me good and *will* do me good; and I say, God bless it!'

5   'Men and women seem by one consent to open their shut-up hearts freely.'

   That is the message of Christmas.

Happy Christmas, everybody!

PRAYER

O God, as we remember at this time the coming of Jesus into this world as a babe at Bethlehem, may we echo the message of the angels: Glory to God in the highest and peace on earth.

NOTES – CHRISTMAS

HOSPITALS

1. We know hospital as place which cares for sick:

    In-patients (residential)
    or Out-patients (non-residential)

2. Word 'hospital' comes from same root as 'hospitality' – the friendly reception of guests.

3. In the UK in 18th and 19th centuries many voluntary hospitals founded by philanthropists (people concerned about wellbeing of others) and staffed by doctors who gave services free.

4. Municipal or town hospitals based on Elizabeth I's Poor Law existed alongside voluntary hospitals until in 1946 both nationalised by **National Health Service Act.**

5. In medieval England sick turned to church for help.
   Monasteries first hospitals.

6. Following story tells of founding of one of London's most famous hospitals:

During the reign of Henry I, Court Jester called **Rahere**. After tragic drowning of heir to throne, Rahere's songs and jokes no longer appreciated. Asked permission to go on pilgrimage to Rome. Months later returned wearing long, dark robe of friar. Friends soon found this was not Rahere the joker. Changed man. Told story to king;

At Rome fallen ill with malaria. For days lay helpless with high fever. Monks of hospital of Three Fountains (Trevi) saved his life. During convalescence had time to think. Had wonderful idea. Would go back to London and build a hospital.

Had vision of St Bartholomew. Rahere claimed he was shown actual site of hospital and church he was to build. Asked King's permission to begin great work at once. Cleared land of stones and weeds. Often mocked by passers-by, but Rahere proclaimed:

'We who are blessed by God with health and wealth should follow in steps of Jesus by helping sick and needy.' St Bartholomew's Hospital opened in 1125. Still stands on same spot in Smithfields (originally called **Smoothfield**, outside City). Rahere's tomb can be seen in part of old priory church. Died in 1144, happy to have repaid his debt to monks who had saved his life in Rome.

PRAYER

Let us ask God's blessing on all who seek to bring health and healing to the sick in our hospitals and on all who serve our community as doctors, health visitors and community carers.

NOTES – HOSPITALS

SIKHISM – GURU TEGH BAHADUR

1. About same time (early December) when Christians thinking of Advent (coming of Jesus) Sikhs remembering martyrdom of 9th Guru – Tegh Bahadur (pronounced Ba-hah-dur). Son of Guru Hargobind (6th Guru).

2. Toured Punjab, Delhi and East India preaching:
    Fatherhood of God
    Brotherhood of Man.

3. Same message as preached by Guru Nanak. (Also notice similarity with teaching of Jesus.)

4. Mughal ruler of that period – Aurangzeb. Majority of subjects Hindus but Aurangzeb was forcing them to be Muslims.

5 Temples demolished – Mosques built in place. Schools were closed and taxes levied on all non-Muslims visiting holy places. Those unable to pay forcibly converted.

6 Group of Hindu Brahmins (priests) heard of Guru Tegh Bahadur and came to him in desperation. Told him of how Hindus' sacred threads were being broken and mark wiped from their forehead. (Both signs very important to Hindus) and being compelled to be Muslims.

7 Guru very upset. Believed only way oppression could be stopped was by sacrifice of holy person.

8 Guru's son said: 'Who is holier than you?'

9 Guru told Brahmins to return home and tell Mughal would only become Muslims if the Guru did also.

10 Obviously then Guru became Mughal's main target but Guru refused to be converted and was executed.

11 Guru's son wrote:

> 'He went to the utmost limit to help the saintly
> He gave his head but never cried in pain.'

12 A Gurdwara (Sikh temple) has been built at place of execution.

13 Remembered by all Sikhs this time of year (early December).

PRAYER

(Part of prayer of Guru Gobind Singh)

> In thee I shall dwell in peace; to dwell in thee is all I wish . . .
> When I have thee, I have everything: Thou, O Lord, art my treasure.

NOTES – SIKHISM-GURU TEGH BAHADUR

PARENTS

1. Years ago Red Indians trained boys very carefully. Every boy dreamed of day when would be called 'a brave'.

    Long, hard period of training.
    Had to be:
    Efficient in war and peace
    Resourceful
    Reliable
    Courageous
    One of the earliest ordeals was **The Vigil**.

2. Boy taken by father deep into forest. Both followed familiar paths at first. Then came to area boy did not know. Village and wigwams now far away. Everything strange.

    Towards sunset, shared a meal. As darkness fell, father said goodbye, turned and left boy alone in forest. Terrified. Hour after hour boy had to keep watch alone, with wild animals prowling and fear of evil spirits. When at last dawn broke, found he'd not been alone. Father had stayed and kept watch with him all night. This secret was never disclosed to other boys.

3. Typical act of a parent. Don't always realise how much we owe to parents.
    Of course, children often grumble about them.
    Find them old-fashioned, restrictive, fuddy-duddy.

4. Story teaches us that the best parents don't DO everything for us but they are always there, helping us to grow up and to do things for ourselves.

5. The bible says 'respect your father and mother' but it also says
    'Parents, do not treat your children in such a way as to make them angry.'

6. There is a responsibility on both sides.

    Parents, like anybody else, have to earn respect.

PRAYER

Give us, O Lord, an understanding of the difficulties that parents face in bringing up their children. And give them an understanding of the difficulties children face in growing up.

NOTES – PARENTS

PETS

(Can begin Assembly by asking students about their pets: cats, dogs, guinea pigs rabbits, canaries, etc.)

1. All pets need care and attention. Parents often complain: 'She/he promised to look after it but I have to do everything – clean it out, feed it, etc.'

2. Most common pets are dogs and cats. Dog called: 'Man's best friend.' Can be very affectionate, very loyal.
    BUT needs training and control.
    (Some dogs are dangerous e.g. attacks on children.)
    Also need exercise.
    Who takes the dog for a walk?

3. Car stickers warn:

    A dog is for life – not for Christmas.

    Sometimes people throw out puppies just after Christmas.
    Some have even been dropped off on motorways and found wandering dangerously.

4. Cats also good companions. Experts say: Stroking a cat reduces stress.
    They also need care and attention. Many get run over and killed.
    Others stolen by criminals for their fur or for animal experiments.

5. Animals have no National Health Service.

    Must be thankful for organisations like:

    (a) RSPCA – Royal Society for Prevention of Cruelty to Animals. (Interestingly received Royal Charter in 1824 when founded. NSPCC founded in 1884 did not.) Has Junior Movement of well over 10,000 members.
    (b) PDSA (People's Dispensary for Sick Animals) formed in 1917 to help poor people who could not afford vets' fees.
    (c) Blue Cross Animal Care. In 1991 cared for 50,000 cats, dogs and other animals at its 16 hospitals, clinics and re-housing branches. Some ill. Some had been run over. Some lost. Worse: many animals simply abandoned.

6. Way we treat animals says great deal about what we are like as people.
    You have to be cruel and heartless to maltreat a dumb, helpless animal.

PRAYER

We thank you, O God for all those who look after and care for animals – veterinary surgeons, the RSPCA, PDSA, Blue Cross and animal homes for dogs, cats and retired horses and donkeys. May we always be kind to animals and be aware how easily we can make them suffer.

NOTES – PETS

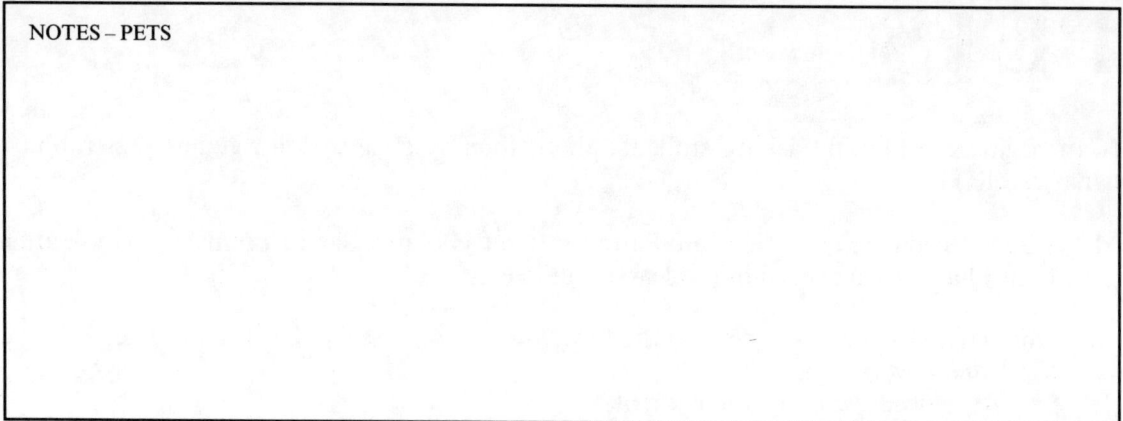

HOME

1   What is a home? Is it just a house or more?

2   French have no word for home. Sometimes use 'le foyer' – hearth, fireside to represent home. Most commonly say: 'Chez nous' – meaning at home, literally 'alongside or with us'.

3   People often described difference between English and French as:

   English – enjoy being at home; 'Englishman's home is his castle.'
   French – prefer to go out e.g. frequently eat out at restaurants.

4   Of course broad generalisations. In any case, people's habits changing. English eat out more often now.

5   What makes a home?
   (a) Somewhere to be together. Doesn't have to be house. Could be tent, shed in the garden.
   (b) Needs basic facilities – to live decently.
   (c) If real home needs people – family, loving relationships.

6   People who have best start in life have caring families – parents, grandparents, etc.

7   But in any family there has to be give and take. Children must also care for their parent or parents and other members of their family.

8   God is often referred to as a father who cares for us. Ideal pattern for fatherhood and motherhood. (God is not a man!)

PRAYER

(Invite assembly to say The Lord's Prayer, remembering students of other religions may wish to remain silent) OR use the words of Bishop Hugh Blackburne:

Let us remember that:
   as many hands build a house
   so, many hearts make a home.

NOTES – HOME

RELIABILITY

1 Jesus told story of two sons:

   Now what do you think? There was once a man who had two sons. He went to the elder one and said, 'Son, go and work in the vineyard today.'
   'I don't want to,' he answered, but later he changed his mind and went.
   Then the father went to the other son and said the same thing.
   'Yes, sir,' he answered, but he did not go.
   Which one of the two did what his father wanted?
   'The elder one', they answered.

2 Sure you recognise situation. Often happens in life. Particularly in families.

3 Sometimes say 'yes' because:
      want to look good
      too weak to be honest.

4 Obviously elder son honest BUT when thought it over knew it was his duty to go.

5 How much do you do at home to help your parents?
   Boys as well as girls need to take share of household chores.

6 But above all be reliable
   Nothing worse than letting someone down.
   Making believe you are going to do something but not actually doing it.

7 In employment, one of most important traits is reliability.

8 It begins at home. Also just as important at school.
   Do teachers regard you as reliable?

9 In fact important everywhere in life.
   Better to be honest and say you are not going to do something than pretend you will and then don't.

   PRAYER

   O, God, We are thankful that we know people who can be trusted and relied upon. Make us in turn reliable and dependable.

NOTES – RELIABILITY

GIVING

1 Giving to other people important part of human life.
   (Not unique to humans. Some animals give and share – particularly to young).

2 Quotation often used:
      'It is more blessed to give than to receive'
      OR, in another translation,
      'There's more happiness in giving than in receiving.'

3 No doubt discovered this for yourself:
      – Finding out what someone wants
        (Better still, thinking of it for yourself).
      – Looking for it in the shops and buying it.
      – Wrapping it up and adding a greeting.
      – Watching the person open it.
      – Sharing in their pleasure.

4 Gives you warm feeling inside.
   Made someone happy.

5   Of course, much more to giving than giving presents.

6   Best giving is when it means sacrifice on our part:
                                 Time
                                 Money
                                 Service

7   Idea of giving at root of many religions e.g.

    ISLAM: One of five pillars on which religion is built is Zakat – the giving of alms (charity) to the poor.
    SIKHISM: One of three types of service is Dhan (money, material)
    JUDAISM: At end of third year Hebrews in O.T. had to give tithe (Tenth Part) of their crops for poor.
    CHRISTIANITY: 'Freely you have received, freely give'.
                                                                                (Matt. 10 v8)

8   Question is not: How much can I spare?
        BUT: What am I prepared to give up?

9   Read story of Widow's Mite (Luke 21 vv1–4)
    and/or the Buddhist story of The Old Woman and the Pomegranate.

One day, Buddha sat under tree to receive presents for poor.
People came from far and near.
First came King Bimbisara: 'Lord Buddha, my gift is the rich
house and lands beyond the river.'
Next came Prince Ajata Shatru: 'Lord Buddha, I bring these valuable jewels.'
Afterwards came many rich lords and merchants with gifts of gold and silver.
Buddha sat and held out his right hand.
Then came an old, thin, bent woman, dressed in rags: 'Lord Buddha, I am a poor woman and have nothing in the world. I was just going to eat this pomegranate. Please, Lord Buddha, take it to the poor. I've nothing else to give.'
At once Lord Buddha stood up and held out both hands to the woman to thank her.
The King, princes, lords and merchants were amazed and said:
'Why did you receive her gift with both hands and stood up to
thank her when you offered us only your right hand and remained
seated?'
'Because', Lord Buddha replied, 'you are all rich men and gave
only a little of what you have but she gave everything.'

PRAYER (St Ignatius Loyola)

Teach us, Good Lord, to serve Thee as Thou deservest;
To give and not to count the cost;
To fight and not to heed the wounds;
To toil and not to seek for rest;
To labour and not to ask for any reward save that of knowing that we do Thy will.

NOTES – GIVING

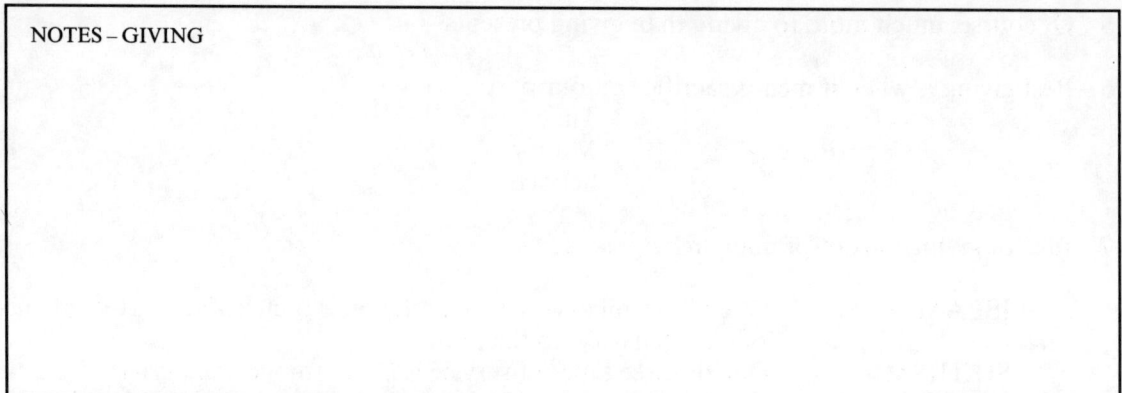

THE TONGUE

1. Have you heard the saying;
   'Sticks and stones may break my bones
   But names will never hurt me'?

2. It isn't true. Calling people names can hurt – very deeply.

3. Don't always realise how damaging the tongue can be. Such a powerful weapon.

4. Listen to the passage from a letter written by James, brother of Jesus, about dangers associated with the tongue

   (Read Letter of James, chapter 3 starting from verse 2, or, if preferred, verse 4, finishing at verse 12.)

5. Tongue needs to be controlled. Can do great deal of harm.

6. Cannot take back what we have said.

   Sometimes say 'I could have bitten my tongue off', but it's too late.

7. Keeping silent very difficult. But better often to wait and think rather than blurt something out.

8. Can you keep a confidence?

   Amusing when people say: 'Keep it to yourself' and then you find they have told everyone else too!

9. Terribly important to be able to be trusted with a confidence. Real test of character.

10. To sum up: Things we say can hurt and hurt badly.

May pride ourselves on being blunt and speaking minds.
There are occasions when we need to speak out. But if it is to individuals then never forget to mix truth with kindness and thoughtfulness.

11 Tongue can also be used to say good, pleasant, complimentary things.

12 Can be tonic. Don't be afraid to compliment. Don't miss opportunity of being generous in praise.

PRAYER:

(In silence, listen to the words of David in Psalm 34 verses 11–14).

Come, my young friends and listen to me.
Would you like to enjoy life? Do you want long life and happiness?
Then hold back from speaking evil and from telling lies.
Turn away from evil and do good.
Strive for peace with all your heart.

NOTES – THE TONGUE

REMEMBRANCE DAY

1 World War 1 finished 11am, 11 Nov 1918.

2 Until after 2nd World War, 2 minutes' silence observed at 11th hour of the 11th month.

3 Then it was changed to second Sunday in November.

4 Best known ceremony is at Cenotaph in Whitehall in London.

Attended by Queen, other members of the Royal Family, leaders of the nations, service chiefs, ambassadors from other countries and representatives of armed services' organisations.

5   Wreaths laid by the Queen, etc. and 'old' soldiers, sailors, airmen march past, proudly wearing medals, badges, berets etc.

6   Not only remembering the dead. Some in wheelchairs or on crutches, reminding us of terrible suffering caused by war.

7   After 1st World War, Commander-in-Chief, Field Marshal Earl Haigh, proposed all ex-servicemen's groups should unite: The British Legion. In 1971 became Royal British Legion.

8   Legion started to sell poppies to raise money to help disabled ex-servicemen. Millions sold every year.

9   Poppy chosen because flowered in battlefields of Belgium.

10 Now we remember dead and disabled of number of wars:

> e.g. 2nd World War
> Korea
> Falklands
> Gulf (Operation Desert Storm)
> etc.

11 At Remembrance Service words of R.L. Binyon repeated:

> 'They shall not grow old as we that are left grow old.
> Age shall not weary them nor the years condemn.
> At the going down of the sun and in the morning
> we shall remember them.'

12 In early days **everybody** stood still for 2 minutes' silence. Cars stopped in streets. Some who didn't had their windscreens broken by angry crowds.

But memories fade and people forget.

13 Let us always be thankful that we have inherited peace and freedom because ordinary people were prepared to sacrifice themselves.

PRAYER:

Rudyard Kipling's verse:

'The tumult and the shouting dies
The captains and the kings depart.
Still stands Thine ancient sacrifice
A humble and a contrite heart.
Lord God of hosts, be with us yet
Lest we forget, lest we forget.'

NOTES – REMEMBRANCE DAY

END OF TERM

1 Last day/week of term/year.
    Seemed long? short?

    Perhaps depends whether student or teacher!

2 Our life divided into little bits:

        modules/lessons
        am/pm
        days/weeks
        months/years.

3 Time can drag:

        when unhappy.
        waiting for big event.

4 Time can fly:

        when enjoying oneself
        on holiday
        at disco
        e.g. a party just flashes by.

5 Time something humans invented.
    Doesn't really exist.
    Can alter it – clocks go forward/backward.
    Can lose/gain time.
    Time human device for convenience.

6 Some people aren't always on time.
    But being on time can be terribly important in life.

7   Sometimes need to stop, switch off, rest.

8   Religions have rest days:

    > Jews – Saturday
    > Muslims – Friday
    > Christians – Sunday (becoming less and less true).

9   Belief is: principle of work **and** rest come from God.

    Need both; God's gifts.
    Need also to learn to use both properly.

10 Rest, recreation (= re-creation). Batteries recharged.

11 Have happy, restful holiday.
    Take time out and return regenerated.

    PRAYER:
    At the end of this term, as we start the holiday, may we find rest for our minds, relaxation for our bodies and peace for our souls.

NOTES – END OF TERM

SIKHISM

(**Setting Scene**: A group of students are visiting a Sikh Temple – called a **Gurdwara**.
Props: A carpet on floor.
         Big book on desk behind which man is sitting.
Actors: Guide – preferably a Sikh
         Man behind desk – preferably a Sikh.
         School party – four students).

(School group arrives from side of stage)

GUIDE: Good morning and welcome. Come this way, please.
Would you take off your shoes and cover your heads? I'll explain why when you have sat down.

(Group sits on carpet with shoes removed and handkerchiefs or scarves on heads).

A: Please tell us why we have to remove our shoes and cover our heads.

GUIDE: It is a sign of respect. Sikhs come to the Gurdwara to think about the deep and holy things of life.

B: Why is the building so empty?

GUIDE: Because Sikhs believe that all are equal. That is why there are no special seats and why we do not have clergymen.

C: But don't you have any leaders?

GUIDE: Yes, they are called Gurus. You may have heard of **Guru Nanak** who was the founder of the Sikh religion.

D: What other Gurus are there?

GUIDE: There were ten in all. The last was **Guru Gobind Singh** who died in 1708. After that there were no more Gurus but their teaching was preserved in our Holy Book which we call the ***Guru Granth Sahib***.

A: Why do Sikhs wear Turbans and have beards?

GUIDE: It goes back to the days when Sikhs were an army. Beards and turbans were their uniform. But Guru Gobind Singh laid it down as a rule that a comb should be worn in the hair which must remain uncut.

B: Are all Sikh men called Singh?

GUIDE: Yes, it is part of their name. Guru Gobind Singh was the one who gave Sikh men the title 'Singh' meaning 'lion' and women 'Kaur' meaning 'princess'.

C: Do Sikhs do anything to help other people?

GUIDE: Yes. Guru Nanak said:
'Work hard and share your earnings'.
Sikhs have set up hospitals and downstairs in all Gurdwaras is a **Langar** which means a Free Kitchen. Food is given, free of charge to anyone who needs it, no matter what religion or race they are.

D: Thank you for all your help. I'm afraid it's time for us to go back to school.

GUIDE: Before you go let me say a Sikh prayer.

PRAYER

(Part of a Sikh Congregational Prayer)
Show us such favour, O Lord, that we by word and deed may belong to you, that in all things we may obtain your assistance and support.

NOTES – SIKHISM

WORLD PROBLEMS

(Take in newspaper or selection of newspapers and read out list of world problems:

      e.g. Famine
        War
        Terrorism
        Poverty
        Global Warming
        etc.

1 Is the world getting any better?
  If not, why not?
  Is it worse?

2 Some say yes, but always been:

      Cruelty
      Robbery
      Murder
      Rape
      War

3 Look at history of human race. Not very pleasant reading.

4 What is the answer?
  Some say education.

  Certainly people need to be made aware of inequalities, injustices, etc.
  Understanding will hopefully result in action.

5 Too often governments are motivated by economic considerations. They say: How will it affect us?

6 Nothing can happen overnight. Changing people's attitudes a huge task.

7 Wonderful story told about Hitler, Mussolini and Churchill who were the leaders of their countries during 1939-45 war.

> All supposed to have met.
> Hitler demanded Churchill sign document saying he had lost war. Refused.
> Suggested wager to settle issue:
> 'See carp in that pool?' said Churchill. 'First one to catch it without using fishing equipment can claim won war.'
> Hitler whipped out his revolver and shot at it but missed.
> Mussolini, being good swimmer, jumped in and tried to catch it but failed.
> Churchill bent down and calmly dipped teaspoon again and again in the water, and threw water over shoulder.
> 'What on earth are you doing?' said Hitler, the Führer.
> 'It will take a long time,' said Churchill 'but we will win in the end.'

8 It is not always the dramatic that wins in end. Sometimes it needs patience.

9 World problems massive but must believe we're going to win in end.

10 Can all play our own small part even if it seems hopeless.

> At rally of 2000 people, all were asked to bring candle. When dark, leader lit his candle. Then, one by one, people present lit theirs.
> Darkness transformed to blazing light.

11 It's all the individual efforts put together that can finally solve world's problems.

PRAYER

Please teach us:

> a proper sensitivity towards Your feeling creation,
> a proper simplicity in the way we live in our environment,
> a proper appreciation of how all people are connected together,
> a proper respect for the well-being of the universe.

NOTES – WORLD PROBLEMS

ISLAM

1. Muslim New Year celebrated on first day of **Muharram**, first month in Muslim calendar.

2. Count year from day of **Hijrat**, which means 'flight'. Commemorates flight of Mohammed from Mecca, where he and his followers were persecuted, to Medina, where he was welcomed in AD 622 (Christian calendar).

    Muslims put AH after number of year.
    1994 AD=1415 AH; 1995 AD=1416 AH.

3. Muslim calendar based on moon's cycle.

    Approximately 11 days shorter than Gregorian Calendar Year established by Pope Gregory XIII in year 1582. Islamic year does not start 1st January.

4. First day of each Muslim month determined by sighting of new moon previous night. (Lunar Month consists of 29 or 30 days).

5. Names of 12 Muslim months are:

    Muharram
    Safar
    Rabi-ul-Awwal
    Rabi-ul-Sani
    Jamadi-ul-Awwal
    Jamadi-ul-Sani
    Rajab
    Shaaban
    Ramadhan
    Shawwal
    Zul 'Qu'adah
    Zul-Hyjah

6. Whilst in Mecca Mohammed was given Holy Book, later known as **Qur'an**, but enemies plotted to kill him.

    In Medina he and companions formed themselves into religious community which spread message of Islam to many other lands.

7. At festival of Hijrat, Muslims worship at mosque and narrate the stories of Mohammed. Perhaps this was one:
    One day Mohammed was travelling with caravan of camels in desert in midday sun. Stopped to rest in shade of some trees. Mohammed tired, fell asleep.
    Sudden shout. Holy Prophet woke to see man standing over him with sword pointing at him.
    Was enemy, idol worshipper who did not believe in one God of Mohammed. Had Mohammed at his mercy.
    Raised sword to strike, saying: 'Who will save you now'?
    Mohammed remained calm. Replied: 'Allah, the one Almighty God will save me'.
    Man astonished to see Mohammed not afraid to be killed.

Sword fell from his hands. Mohammed quickly picked it up and grabbed attacker, saying 'And who can save *you*'?
Terrified man thinking his last hour had come replied:
'Only you can save me.'
Mohammed let man go.
Man now knew meaning of mercy. Became Muslim and followed teachings of Mohammed all his life.

PRAYER (Part of Muslim prayer recited every day).

> Guide along the straight way –
> The way of those You have favoured
> and not of those who earn Your anger
> nor of those who go astray.

NOTES – ISLAM

END OF SCHOOL YEAR

1 Another school year coming to an end.

> Flown by?
> Dragged?

2 Depends on attitude:

> Regret: Not having used time more profitably
> Enjoyable experiences passed so quickly
> e.g. school trip/s, concerts, matches, Sports Day, sponsored events, etc.
> Happy: Revision and exams completed,
> Break from routine of school day,
> Rest from getting up early for school
> Looking forward to holidays – going away?

3 All need break from routine:

> Change is as good as a rest.

4 Rest itself important too for both mind and body.
Ideal is 'mens sanis in corpore sano' ('Healthy mind in a healthy body')
Rest repairs our bodies and renews our minds.

5   No doubt in holidays you will sometimes just laze about.
    Hopefully also have opportunity to go right away and forget school and all your worries.

6   Holidays for some can be bore and a drag.
    Parents continue to work.
    Do not go away.
    Children left at home saying: 'What can we do?'

7   Don't forget:

    Parks
    Swimming pools
    Skating rinks
    Bowling alleys
    Canals
    Rivers   Use ones appropriate to
    Museums   School area.
    Theatres   Add other facilities
    Cinemas etc.   available.

8   There are holiday activities,
    (Quote from local pamphlets. Some may actually take place in school.)

9   School holidays can be time of problems for parents, community and police.
    Old saying: 'The Devil finds mischief for idle hands to do'.

10 Don't get into trouble in holidays.

    Use time profitably. Derive benefit from break.
    Don't just hang around looking for mischief.
    Be able to say: 'It was a lovely holiday'.

11 Thank you to all who have made this a happy year: (Specify)

12 Have happy holiday.

    Let's ask God's blessing on it:

    PRAYER

    We look in thankfulness at all the good experiences of this year. We ask your blessing on us as we look forward to the holidays. Grant that we may renew our minds and bodies and help us to enjoy ourselves without making others unhappy.

NOTES – END OF SCHOOL YEAR

LEAVERS' ASSEMBLY

1. Time at school coming to end:

    > Some sad
    > Others can't wait.

2. School important. School matters despite constant **denigration** by all and sundry.

3. Significant part of our lives.

    Michael Rutter (and others) published book in 1979:
    > 'Fifteen Thousand Hours'

    Represents approx. time spent in school from 5 yrs–16yrs.

4. What has school done for you?
   I'll tell you what we have tried to do:

    (a) Inculcate knowledge.
        You will have learned important facts. Content often despised these days but as adults, you will need to be able to share knowledge in order to enjoy full life.
    (b) Develop processes and skills.
        Knowledge can be useless unless we have skills to use it.
        Above all need skills to 'learn how to learn' – sometimes called 'Information Skills'.
    (c) Introduce you to privileges and responsibilities of community life that will also apply to wider world outside.

5. Trust you will also have developed independence of thought;
    > Able to solve problems;
    > Make informed decisions.

6. And whilst here, hopefully, will have learned that people are far more important than anything else;

    > Good relationships
    > Give and take needed to get on with other people.

7. Hope you will have learned great deal about yourself:
    > Capabilities
    > Limitations

   Because you carry yourself through all stages of your life;
   Others (teachers, friends) can come and go.
   Above all, know yourself.

8. Hope all will look back on school as enjoyable experience.

9. Good Luck and Best Wishes.

Whatever you do next (college, employment, etc): Wish you every success.

10 Some, unfortunately, may be unemployed. Try to be patient.

Persevere. Never turn down any opportunity.
Don't forget you'll probably be judged more on what you are than exams you've passed.

11 (Optional Ending. Recital of part of Psalm 23 – Good News Version)

> The Lord is my shepherd. I have everything I need.
> He lets me rest in fields of green grass and leads me
> to quiet pools of fresh water.
> He gives me new strength. He guides me in the right paths, as
> He has promised.
> Even if I go through the deepest darkness, I will not be
> afraid, Lord, for You are with me.
> Your shepherd's rod and staff protect me. . . .
> I know that Your goodness and love will be with me all my
> life, and Your house will be my home as long as I live.

NOTES – LEAVERS' ASSEMBLY

SELFLESSNESS

1 (Begin assembly by citing current/recent/past disaster e.g. aeroplane crashing, train accident, terrorist bomb, etc.)

2 Hours of painstaking, selfless work by firemen, ambulance workers, doctors, nurses, etc.

Also by ordinary citizens – passengers, passers-by, residents, etc.

3 Without thought for themselves, people plunge into dangerous places e.g. with falling masonry, risk of fire, smoke-filled rooms.

4 Afterwards some can't believe they have done it.

Out of character, not normally brave;
No time for thinking – just did it.

5   Also must remember that some suffer terrible trauma as result of experience:

> e.g. firemen in King's Cross disaster
> (Use own examples)

6   Often at scene of disaster will see Salvation Army Canteen.

7   During war Salvationists served troops from their canteens often in dangerous places near front line.

8   Salvation Army remarkable organisation.

Formed in 1865 by Rev. William Booth.
Adopted name Salvation Army in 1878.

9   Called followers 'army' because fighting for God against evil.

So, wear uniform, have officers, call churches citadels and magazine called Warcry.

10   Salvation Army also known as: 'Army of Helping Hand'.

11   Wherever there is need the SA is there.

Has schools, hospitals, orphanages, old peoples' homes, holiday homes.

12   Every night SA personnel tour streets of cities distributing soup to people sleeping rough.

13   Famous for 'Missing Persons' Branch.

Anybody can contact it about missing members of family.
Extremely well organised. Has great success in thousands of cases.

14   SA not only people who do this work but typical of those who offer 'helping hand'.

15   What are you doing?

> e.g. helping old person with shopping
> changing library books for housebound
> doing garden for disabled.

PRAYER:

Make us aware of the needs of those worse off than ourselves, especially old people living on their own. May we offer a helping hand, thinking, not of ourselves, but of others.

NOTES – SELFLESSNESS

WORK

1. Latin phrase sometimes used as motto:
   >LABOR OMNIA VINCIT. (Work conquers everything).

2. Perhaps now considered out of date.

   3,000,000 unemployed? (Give current figure)
   Students in some areas with 5 GCSE passes A-C not finding jobs.
   As bad for some graduates.

3. Motto never been entirely true:

   >Some people made slaves by cruel mine and factory bosses. Worked shockingly long hours for pittance.
   >e.g. children in mines
   >   mill workers.

4. Nevertheless, work conquering everything is a good general principle:

   >Good workers: appreciated
   >   noticed
   >   promoted.

   Of course, exceptions. Some people unfairly treated.

5. Certainly the saying: 'There is no substitute for hard work' is true for most students. Some seem to sail through on brains alone but most have to work for success.
   For advanced studies e.g. 'A' Level, if you wish to succeed, you *have* to work. Brains alone are not enough.

6. People blame our obsession with work on Protestant 'work ethic'.

   All brought up to believe work is necessary and God's will for us.

7. Willingness to work *does* have something to do with character – not necessarily paid work. Work in general.
   Using energy, working at something.

8. Effort required to work. Effort quite separate from ability.

9. That's why school reports have two grades;
   >   'Effort and Attainment.'
   >(Say what's appropriate for your report format or if
   > not applicable, simply refer to importance of effort).

10. Effort is often more important than attainment.
    Point is: Are you doing as much as you are able?

11 Employers, colleges and universities usually want to know how much candidate is prepared to work, as well as what exams they have passed.

12 No, work doesn't conquer everything But there is great deal of truth in it. Can contribute to success. Lack of it can bring failure.

13 Let's spend last few minutes thinking about what the writer of The Book of Proverbs (in the O.T.) said about people who are lazy:

> Lazy people should learn a lesson from the way ants live.
> They have no leader, chief or ruler, but they store up their food during the summer, getting ready for the winter.
> How long is the lazy man going to lie in bed? When is he ever going to get up?
> 'I'll just take a short nap', he says; 'I'll fold my hands and rest a while'.
> But while he sleeps, poverty will attack him like an armed robber.

NOTES – WORK

CHRISTMAS DECORATIONS AND PREPARATIONS

1 Long before Christian Christmas, people gathered evergreens in December.
Decorated homes and temples to drive away evil spirits.
Early Christians continued custom giving it Christian meaning.

2 HOLLY: Used to be called 'holm'.
  Different Christian interpretations:
  One story:
  Holly tree outside stable where Christ was born. Had no berries. Been eaten by birds.
  To honour Christ's birth bore buds, flowers and berries all in one night.
  Prickly holly leaves supposed to represent crown of thorns and red berries Christ's blood.

3 MISTLETOE: Part of Pagan New Year ceremonies.
That's why not used in churches.
However, in York Minister there was special mistletoe ceremony where wrongdoers could come to receive pardon.
Became emblem of love since its berries are evergreen and grow in pairs.

4 ROSEMARY: Now used mainly for cooking.
Used to be favourite decoration because of attractive green spikes and fragrant smell.

5 IVY: Romans thought ivy had magic powers.
Used ivy to make crowns and wreaths to honour gods and victorious generals.

6 YULE LOG: Used to be brought home and put in position on hearth. Lit from piece of last year's log specially saved.

(Yule = Yuletide = pagan Midwinter Festival.
Now mainly preserved in a Christmas chocolate cake made in form of log).

7 Midnight on Christmas Eve time for Midnight Mass and for ringing of church bells, announcing death of Devil and birth of Christ.

8 Midnight also time (according to legend) when animals speak like humans and bees hum in praise of Christ.

9 Lovely carol about meaning of holly for Christmas is:
'The Holly and the Ivy'

(Can be sung by assembly as carol, performed by soloist or choir or read).

PRAYER

We thank you, O God, for the yearly message of the child born in a stable and for the hope that comes to us at Christmastime. Help us to be more honest with ourselves and more loving towards our fellow human beings.

NOTES – CHRISTMAS DECORATIONS AND PREPARATIONS

MAUNDY THURSDAY

1. Crucifixion of Jesus remembered on Good Friday (Good = Holy).

2. Day before called Maundy Thursday.

   'Maundy' comes from Latin 'mandatum' = command.

3. On that Thursday Jesus invited disciples to supper.
   Now referred to as Last Supper.

   Before supper Jesus washed feet of disciples.
   (Roads very dusty in Palestine. Custom for servant to wash feet of guests before meal.)

4. Told disciples they should do same for one another.
   Also gave them new Commandment:
   > 'Love one another as I have loved you.'
   (Hence command = mandatum = Maundy).

5. At meal Jesus took some bread and wine and told disciples these represented his body and blood.
   (He was referring to his death).
   Asked them to remember him when they had such a meal together.

   Note: bread and wine were normal meal at that time.
   (Read full account in John 13 vv1–18).

6. Today this meal is held regularly in many churches.
   Is called by various names:
   > e.g. Communion
   > Eucharist
   > Mass
   > Lord's Supper
   > Breaking of Bread.

7. Church leaders, eg Pope and kings have continued practice of washing feet of others.

8. However James II last king of England to do this.
   Since then, King or Queen have presented old people with Maundy money.
   Equal number of men and women recipients, each group representing age of monarch.
   All given two purses – one red and one white.
   Red contains Maundy money – specially minted silver coins in sets of 4,3,2,1 pence.
   > e.g. when Queen Elizabeth II was 65,
   > each person given 6 complete sets plus 3p and 2p coins.
   White purse contains ordinary coin of realm in lieu of food which used to be given.

9 Jesus taught importance of service and humility. He himself refused to be treated as someone special, preferring to regard himself as a servant. Christians try to follow his example.

PRAYER

Serving Christ In One Another
(Poem by Susan Appleby).

You told us
to wash
each other's feet, Lord
as you did.

Did you not know
that we would
have baths –
wear closed shoes –
drive cars –
have metalled roads, Lord?

You opened
deaf ears
blind eyes
bowed
proud hearts –
I hear, Lord
I see
and give myself
to you
in washing other's feet.

On my knees
on their behalf, Lord –
Praying.
Too low
to judge
to criticise.
Vulnerable
to kicks
Vulnerable
to hurt
Vulnerable . . .

But that is what love is, Lord –
pride goes
self goes
fear goes –
and I learn
to serve you.

NOTES – MAUNDY THURSDAY

GOOD FRIDAY AND EASTER SUNDAY

1. At one time called God's Friday.

   Day Jesus was crucified by Romans in Jerusalem.

2. Had angered Jewish leaders by challenging their authority.
   Wanted opportunity to arrest him but Jesus was elusive . . .

3. Judas Iscariot, one of twelve disciples, betrayed him to Caiaphas, High Priest. Told him Jesus would be in Garden of Gethsemane.
   Judas identified Jesus for Temple Police by kissing him.
   Received 30 pieces of silver for deed. Hanged himself later.

4. Jesus put in front of unofficial meeting of Jewish Council, (Sanhedrin).

   When challenged as to whether Messiah, replied 'I am'.

5. Accused of blasphemy and judged worthy of death.

6. Early on Friday morning verdict ratified at official Sanhedrin meeting.

7. Sanhedrin had no power to execute Jesus because Romans ruled at time.

8. Jesus sent to Pilate, Roman Procurator of Judea and Samaria.

9. Pilate found Jesus innocent of charge but acceded to cries of mob for crucifixion.

10. Pilate saw one last chance. Custom to release one prisoner at Passover. Thought crowd would choose Jesus rather than Barrabas, convicted political agitator and murderer. They chose Barrabas.

11 Pilate, unable to save Jesus, asked for bowl of water, washed his hands, saying:

> 'I wash my hands of this innocent man's blood'.

12 Jesus taken to Golgotha ('Skull') – a skull-shaped hill outside walls of Jerusalem.

13 One of last utterances was:

> 'Father forgive them for they know not what they do'.

14 On cross 3 hours from 12 noon till 3pm.
Many churches hold special services lasting from 12 to 3pm on Good Friday.

15 Taken from cross and laid in cave, in garden belonging to Joseph of Arimathea.

16 On Sunday (according to account in John's Gospel chap 20):

Mary Magdalen came to the garden early, and saw a man who said: 'Why are you crying? Who are you looking for?'
Thinking he was the gardener, she said:
'If you have taken him away, tell me where you have put him and I will go and get him.'
Jesus said to her: 'Mary.'
She turned to him and said in Hebrew: 'Rabboni', which means 'Teacher'.
Jesus told her to go and tell the others that he was alive.
She then went and told them she had seen the Lord.

17 This event is remembered in Christian Church on Easter Sunday.

PRAYER

(Verse of well known Good Friday Hymn.
Whole hymn may be recited or sung.
Alternatives like: 'There is a green hill far away' may be preferred).

'When I survey the wondrous cross
On which the Prince of Glory died
My richest gain I count but loss
And pour contempt on all my pride.'

NOTES – GOOD FRIDAY AND EASTER SUNDAY

WHITSUN

1. Fifty days after Easter is Whitsun.
   Short for Whit Sunday.
   Originally called White Sunday as was popular day for baptism of Christian adults who wore white baptismal gowns.

2. People wanted to be baptised because Whit Sunday regarded as Church's birthday when Christians believe Holy Spirit was given to disciples.

   (Account found in Acts of Apostles chapter 2 either verses 1–13 or 1–21).

3. Baptism and Holy Spirit connected in Christianity,

   e.g. Jesus said to Nicodemus:
   'No-one can enter the Kingdom of God unless he is born of water and the Spirit.'

4. Water represents washing away of one's sins
   Holy Spirit, for Christian, gives power to start new life.
   Jesus called this: 'being born again'.

5. Whitsun sometimes referred to as Pentecost – this is Greek meaning 50th day.

   Pentecost comes 50 days after the Jewish Festival of Passover which fell on Friday Jesus was crucified.

6. Date for Whitsun different every year.
   Depends on Easter which is moveable feast (determined by phases of moon).

7. Spring holiday used to take place at Whitsun.

   In order to make intervals between holidays more equal, Spring holiday now fixed for end of May, beginning of June.
   (There is even talk of fixing Easter to be same every year but many Christians want to keep actual anniversary).

8. Whitsun traditionally holiday (holy day).

   Celebrated with Morris dancing, fairs, etc.
   In Middle Ages custom to perform Miracle or Mystery Plays.
   Portrayed events from Bible.
   Still performed at Chester, York and Coventry.

PRAYER

Let us remember the message of Whitsuntide, that the Spirit of God can give us the power to transform our lives and begin anew with courage and confidence.

NOTES – WHITSUN

PEACEMAKING – ARCHBISHOP DESMOND TUTU

1. Born in district of Transvaal in S. Africa.
   Tribally mixed parentage:
           Xhosa father
           Motswana mother.

2. Under laws of Apartheid*, passport stated nationality as:
           'Undetermined at present'.
   *(Apartheid – Past Racial Policy of Government of S Africa between 1948 and 1992 under which White, African, Asiatic and Coloured communities were segregated).

3. As black child remembered seeing friends scavenging in dustbins of 'white' school to find remnants of unwanted school lunches.

4. At senior school in Johannesburg greatly influenced by Father Trevor Huddleston – one of leaders of Anti-Apartheid Movement.

5. Won place at Medical School but family could not afford it. Instead, studied for BA at all-black college in Pretoria.

6. Taught 4 years in secondary schools.
   Married another teacher, Leah.
   Left teaching when Bantu Education Act dictated blacks should only be educated for 'Basic Labour'.

7. Aged 25, attended Anglican Theological College in Johannesburg.
   Then studied divinity at King's College, London.

8 1962: Returned to S Africa to lecture on theology.
   1965: Came back to London to work for World Council of Churches.
   1975: Became first black Dean of Jonannesburg Cathedral.
   Short while Bishop of the Diocese of Lesotho (formerly Basutoland).
   Then elected General Secretary of South African Council of Churches.

9 Used position to attack Apartheid.
   Angered Government. Commission set up to look into activities of Council of Churches.

10 Desmond Tutu awarded Nobel Peace Prize in 1984.
   Accepted on behalf of:

   'All those people whose noses are rubbed into the dust every day'.

   Polls showed 75% of white S Africans disapproved of award.

11 In 1986 made Archbishop of Capetown.

12 Tutu totally against violence.
   Regarded now as world figure of mediation and reconciliation.
   Attacks vigorously with words, warning opponents against taking on The Church of God – reminding them of fate of:
   Nero, Hitler, Idi Amin of Uganda.

13 Tutu is man of peace. A peacemaker who many see as one of few figures in S Africa who has held back violence against State.

THOUGHT FOR DAY

Jesus said:
'Happy are those who work for peace; God will call them His children'.

NOTES – PEACEMAKING

OFFERING HELP AND ADVICE

1. Story told of man who had three sons.
   Decided in his will would leave:
   > half his camels to eldest
   > a third to middle son
   > a ninth to youngest.

2. Unfortunately, on death, there were only 17 camels.
   Could not be divided by 2, 3, or 9.

3. Neighbour heard of predicament. Came to rescue.
   Gave brothers 1 camel making 18.

4. So:
   > the eldest had 9
   > the next had 6
   > and the youngest had 2.

5. Which left 1 over which brothers gratefully returned to neighbour.

6. Sometimes need outsider to solve our problem.

   Basis of counselling: person who is neutral, objective, not involved in situation.
   Can see things more clearly, has no axe to grind.

7. Great need for counsellors, advisers.
   Individuals with sympathetic ear and time to give.

8. Can cost, but story of camels shows often there is a reward, a return which makes it all worthwhile.

PRAYER

Prevent us, O Lord, from always thinking that we must be self-sufficient. May we be prepared to accept advice and help when it is needed.

NOTES – OFFERING HELP AND ADVICE

HINDUISM – HOLI

1. Holi most colourful of Hindu Festivals.
   Spring Festival celebrated in India on full moon day of month of Phalgun, (Feb–Mar).

2. Legends says:
   Mighty King – Hiranya Kashipu – once ruled earth.
   Grew very arrogant. Announced he was a god.
   Ordered subjects to worship him.

3. Prahad, only son of King, refused to obey.
   King punished him and tried to kill him.
   Prahad saved each time by uttering name of Vishnu (Preserver, – one of three most important Hindu gods Others: Brahma – Creator; Siva – Destroyer).

4. Finally, Prahad's aunt, claiming to be fireproof, took him on her lap and sat on fire.
   Flames died down: aunt burnt alive; Prahad safe and sound.

5. Festival time of singing and dancing.
   Lasts from 3–5 days. Carnival atmosphere – street dancing and processions. Bright clothes worn.

6. Pranks are also played
   People remember story of Lord Krishna hiding clothes of cow-girls when bathing and how milkmaids sprayed people with coloured powder.

7. At night bonfires lit with images of Holika – the wicked aunt.

PRAYER: (Described by Hindu source as the main Hindu prayer).

> O God! You are the giver of life,
> The healer of pains and sorrows,
> The giver of happiness.
> O Creator of the Universe,
> Send us your purifying light
> And lead our thoughts in your ways.

HINDUISM – HOLI

HUNGER

1. According to latest Food and Agricultural Organisation (FAO) of UN survey:

    - over 780 million people in world undernourished.
      (More than population of Europe).
    - nearly 13 million children die every year as
      direct result of hunger, malnutrition and infections
    - most of hungry in Asia
      (in S Asia more than 100 million children underweight)

2. Malnutrition in individual affects:

    - growth and reproduction
    - health
    - learning capacity
    - activity
    - overall quality of life and well-being.

3. Conversely, overnutrition contributes to diet-related diseases:
    e.g. heart disease, adult diabetes and some cancers.

4. Body mass index (BMI) simple indicator of fatness or thinness.
   Higher the number bigger (and presumably fatter) you are.
   Conversely, low number indicates thinness.

5. BMI calculated by:

    - taking weight in kilograms

    - dividing it by height in metres squared.
      e.g. weight 60 kg ÷ 1.6 × 1.6 (60÷2.56) = 23.4

   Over 25 is overweight; below 18.5 underweight with some risk.

6. By collecting and monitoring these statistics, FAO provides information to countries on nutritional state of their people and levels of food security.

7. Globally enough food for all.

   BUT need is for food security i.e. ensuring all people at all times have access to food they need for healthy life.
   Food must be physically and economically accessible.

8. For everyone to have equal share need for long-term commitment from everybody:
    individuals
    nations
    members of international community.

9 Resources and expertise required from all sectors;
- government and industry
- farmers and consumers
- scientists
- AND countless thousands who prepare food.

10 Knowledge about nutrition essential.
Education and information materials provide that knowledge.
Achieved by gathering and furnishing of statistics and impact of mass media:
promoting low-cost nutritious foods and generating pressure by reporting early warning signs of trouble.

11 Everyone in world entitled to healthy diet.
Should also be concern to us if we wish to enjoy long and happy life.
How healthy is your diet?

PRAYER

We know that what matters most in life is not money or our age but our health.
Remembering those in the world who do not have enough to eat or do not enjoy a nutritious diet, help us to be thankful for the benefits we enjoy in this country that we may learn to live and eat wisely and healthily.

NOTES – HUNGER

THREE CHINESE FESTIVALS

A. CHING MING – Tomb-sweeping Festival in Spring.

1. Tidying family graves one of oldest customs in Chinese Book of Folklore.
   From early morning visit tombs of ancestors.
   Take incense, joss paper and buns specially baked for dead.

2. Sweep tombs. Weed, plant new tree and repaint faded inscriptions.
   Joss paper scattered round tombs as sign of respect.
   (Not usually celebrated in Britain).

B. **THUAN YANG** – Dragon-boat Festival.

    3 Most colourful and exciting of Chinese traditional festivals.
       Commemorates hero of 3rd cent BC. Drowned himself in protest against bad government.

    4 Races take place on river with musicians and fireworks.

    5 Competitors usually young men living on opposite banks of river.
       Build own boats. Brightly coloured with dragon heads and tails.

    6 Great deal of noise and splashing representing attempts to rescue hero.

    7 Seen as challenge between people from opposite banks.
       Winners presented with huge banners decorated with golden dragon.

C. **CHUNG YANG** – Also called Double Nine because celebrated on 9th day of 9th Moon.

    8 Legend says:

          Two friends travelled together for many years pursuing studies.
          One day one had premonition;
          on 9th day of 9th Moon grave disaster would strike friend's family.
          Could be avoided if family left home and spent day in hills.

    9 Friend and family accepted advice.
       Returned home at nightfall. All animals had died.
       Believed they would have died too.

   10 Custom at this Double Nine for Chinese to climb hills, towers or Pagodas.
       Also called 'Day of Ascending Heights'.

   11 Chrysanthemum wine and dishes served as delicacy.
       (Chrysanthemums in full bloom at this time of year).

THOUGHT (from the Analects of Confucius):

'The higher type of man seeks all that he wants in himself.
    The inferior man seeks all that he wants from others'.

NOTES – THREE CHINESE FESTIVALS

HONESTY

1. Many people pride themselves on honesty.

   Say: would never steal/rob/cheat.

2. But how honest are they really?

   How honest are you? how honest am I?
   – Deep down I mean.

3. (Show assembly wallet or purse).

   Say I dropped this on way out of hall.
   What would you do?
   Pick it up? Give it back to me?
   Probably. But why?
   – because others are watching?
   – because it belongs to me and you know me?
   – because you are always honest?

4. Say I dropped my wallet in corridor and you didn't know whose it was.

   What would you do? Hand it in to school office/teacher?

5. Some would. Perhaps because found in school.

   Sense of duty; loyalty to community in which live
   (Quote any recent example of such honesty in school).

6. Now, say, you found wallet full of money in gutter:

   – don't know whose it is
   – nobody else around.

7. What do you do?
   – Pop it in pocket/bag?
   – Take it into park, empty it and throw wallet away?
   – Hand it to police station or school?

8. Perhaps depends on how much in wallet.

   It's said: Everybody has his/her price.
   Would you commit a crime for 10p? £5?
   What about £1000? Or if someone offered you £100,000?
   No? Well what about £1,000,000? Not so sure?

9   Easy to pretend money doesn't matter

   Basis of modern society.
   Much more complex now:
       FT Index
       Price of mark/dollar/yen.
       Stocks and shares (for many more people e.g. BT, Gas, etc).

10 People say: 'All we want is enough to live on'.
   But how much is enough? Most of us want more than we have.

11 In society so dominated by money we can easily be tempted to try to obtain it by dishonest means.
   We then justify ourselves by saying, for example:
       'Everybody does it' or 'Burglary doesn't hurt anybody, insurance will pay!'

12 Always need to take great care with money – our own as well as others'.

13 Money needs to be shared with others:
   to be means to end rather than end in itself.

   PRAYER:
   Let us think for a moment how we live our lives.
   May we appreciate the truth of the saying:
   'Honesty is the best policy'.

   NOTES – HONESTY

BEING THANKFUL

1   Easy to grumble:
       – weather
       – homework
       – parents
       – school
       – lack of money etc.

2   What about good things?

    Count your blessings. You say you haven't any?
    Perhaps one or more of these:
    – good health?
    – caring parent/s?
    – comfortable home?
    – good school? (staff, facilities)

3   So easy to take things for granted.

    Often only realise value of something when we lose it (e.g. health, home)

4   Important not just to *be* thankful
    but *say* thank-you.

5   Saying thank-you therapeutic.

    Heals, cures, makes people feel better.

6   Sometimes say to students: 'Did you say thank-you?'
    They say: 'No, but it was understood.'
    Was it? Not necessarily so.
    No substitute for actually *saying* it.

7   How pleasant it is when students after school trip remember to say thank-you. Some even write note.

8   Good custom after match to give three cheers to other side.
    Acknowledges sporting competition.
    Whether winners or losers, saying thank-you for good, enjoyable game.

9   Saying thank-you makes everybody feel happy:
    those who say it
    and those who are thanked.

10 In past, schools sometimes finished term/year with hymn:

    'Now thank we all our God
    With heart and hands and voices.'

11 So much to be thankful for – blessings from God and good things of life around us.

    PRAYER (Another hymn – adapted)

    We praise God for:
    The beauty of the earth
    The beauty of the skies
    The love which from our birth
    over and around us lies.

>(PAUSE)

For:
The joy of human love,
Brother, sister, parent, child,
Friends . . .
>(PAUSE)

For:
The joy of ear and eye
The heart and mind's delight.

NOTES – BEING THANKFUL

WATER

1. One of basic needs of human beings – water.

   (Suggest = sip from glass of water).

2. Easy to take it for granted. Water shortage over last few years in this country has made us think more seriously.

3. How many of us just let the tap run?

   In Britain:

   > Average daily amount of water used = 30 Galls.
   > Made up of:
   > (a) Washing and having baths =11 Galls.
   > (b) Drinking, cooking, washing up, laundry and flushing lavatory =19 Galls.

4. 150 years ago only 4 Galls used per person.
   By year 2000 estimated 50 Galls.

5. See pictures almost every day on TV or in newspapers of people, animals, crops dying from drought in other parts of world.

46

6 STORY:

> Couple – man and wife – from Britain went to live in Africa.
> Where stayed rained only 2 months of year.
> Had tank of water on roof holding 40 Galls.
> **THIS FOR EVERYTHING UNTIL NEXT RAINS.**
> (Remember our 30 Galls PER DAY!)
>
> Donkeys passed every day with goat-skins of water on back. Sold it by pint.
> Group of passing traders on camels stopped outside door of couple. Called for water.
> **ONE NEVER REFUSES WATER IN AFRICA.**
> Servant took out jug. Each drank in turn.
> Wife hoped some water would remain.
> But last one poured remainder on ground,

7 Angrily, woman asked servant why.

   Replied: 'It's their way of being thankful to God for water'.

8 Water is sacred to Hindus.
   Jews and Hindus wash before eating.
   Muslims wash thoroughly before entering mosque.

9 Water is precious. We need to treat it with more respect and use it more economically.

10 But what can we do to help areas of drought?
   Can send them food but drums of water almost impossible task.

   Answer is:
   – Technical advice to find water supplies
   – Training
   – Expertise
   – Equipment for drilling, etc.

   PRAYER

   We give thanks for rain, rivers and streams and for the water from our taps.
   May we not only *think* about people who have no water but *do* something positive to help.

NOTES – WATER

SPRING

(You need a flower arrangement on table/lectern. This needs to be done by someone who is skilful at flower arranging, ideally but not essentially, in Japanese Ikebana style).

1. Winter favourite season for some:

    – Find attraction in cosiness of dark evenings at home in warmth and light.
    – Cold, they say, makes them more energetic.

2. Most people can't wait for winter to end:

    – Long dark days over.
    – Sun getting brighter and hotter.
    – World of Nature coming back to life.

3. Shoots re-appear and flowers begin to grow.

    One of great pleasures of Spring is beauty of flowers.
    (Point out details of flowers on display:
    – colour
    – shape
    – scent.

4. There is popular children's hymn often sung at Springtime:
    'All things bright and beautiful'.
    You may remember it from your Junior/Middle School days.

5. One verse is:

    'Each little flower that opens,
    Each little bird that sings,
    He (God) made their glowing colours,
    He made their tiny wings.'

6. Another hymn says:
    'He paints the wayside flower.'

7. These poetic descriptions remind us of greatness of God:
    Seen in small delicate flowers, birds and insects just as much as in mighty mountains, seas, sun, moon and stars.

8. Next time you go into country, look for and try to identify wild flowers.

    (BUT DO NOT PICK THEM. LEAVE THEM FOR EVERYBODY'S PLEASURE).

9. Look at flowers in this vase/display. Been skilfully arranged.

Art of flower arranging learnt from Japanese.
Gave it name: IKEBANA (keeping flowers alive).

10. Ikebana originated in Buddhist worship.
Lotus flower offered as gift to Buddha.

11. Ikebana an arrangement with three levels.
Represent: heaven, human beings and earth.

12. Flower arranging is skilful art.
Worth studying for girls *and* boys.

13. Skilful flower arrangements add beauty and colour to church services, particularly at time of Spring Festivals.

PRAYER:

Let us give thanks for the beauty of Nature and especially for flowers as they break into blossom at this time.
Help us to respect the countryside so that it may continue to be enjoyed by all.

NOTES – SPRING

SWORD OF DAMOCLES

1. Legend says:

   Damocles, courtier of Dionysius (405–367BC), tyrant of Syracuse, spoke extravagantly about wonderful life of Dionysius.
   Imagined he was happiest man in world – wealthy and powerful.
   Dionysius invited Damocles to sumptuous banquet to enjoy happiness he so much envied.
   Seated him beneath naked sword suspended from ceiling by single thread.
   Damocles afraid to stir. Banquet tantalising torment to him.
   Thus tyrant demonstrated fortune of people who hold power is as precarious as predicament in which he placed guest.

2. Sword of Damocles has become symbol of impending evil or danger.

   Everybody, at any time, in danger of accidents, misfortunes or reversal of fortunes.

3   This should not make us pessimistic or nervous about future.

   BUT we need to have understanding of balance of life:

   – good and evil
   – good luck and misfortune
   – joy and sorrow.

4   No-one can escape ups and downs of life, however wealthy or powerful.

5   Must not be complacent.

   Must build up inner resources of will and strength of mind and spirit.

6   Many find belief in God helps in facing changing fortunes of life.
   Prayer gives religious people channel for gaining strength and confidence.

7   For them, life is not game of chance but journey in company of God.

   PRAYER (Famous words of M.L. Haskins):
   'Go out into the darkness and put your hand into the hand of God.
   That shall be to thee better than light and safer than a known way.'

NOTES – SWORD OF DAMOCLES

MOTHERING SUNDAY

1   Celebrated 4th Sunday of Lent.
   Only day in Lent historically when allowed break from fast.

2   Term originally referred to *mother* church (church of one's parish).
   People away from home, particularly servants, returned and went to church together.

3   Gradually Mothering Sunday became centred on the 'Mother'.

   Family brought her gifts – trinkets, flowers, cakes.
   (Special cake – SIMNEL – rich fruit cake with layer of marzipan and decorated – eaten during Lent and Easter).

4   Ask members of other religions if they celebrate a Mother's Day:

   e.g. popular Hindu festival, Dashara, is family festival.
        also kind of Mother's day.

5   Survey by Legal and General Insurance published early 1993 claims housewives have equal right with husbands to be called breadwinners.

6   Calculated cost of employing someone to do mother's job for a week:

   (These could be shown on overhead projector).

JOB	HOURS	RATE	TOTAL
Nanny	17.9	£5.90	£105.61
Cook	12.2	£5.35	£65.27
Cleaner	12.2	£5.35	£65.27
Laundress	9.3	£3.80	£35.34
Shopper	6.4	£3.80	£24.32
Dishwasher	5.7	£3.80	£21.66
Driver	2.6	£4.50	£11.70
Gardener	1.4	£5.90	£8.26
Seamstress	1.7	£3.60	£6.12
Other	1.3	£4.00	£5.20
TOTALS	70.7		£348.75

7   Quite staggering.

   Of course, these days many dads share housework:
         – cooking, cleaning, gardening, ironing, shopping, etc.

   Conversely, mums share breadwinning by going out to work.

8   Quite high percentage of homes now with one parent where mum or dad have to play both roles.

9   But many homes still very dependent on Mum.

10 Let us give thanks for our mums and dads and for all they do for us.

   PRAYER

   Thank God for our parents and specially for Mum.
   May we always be helpful and considerate in the home.
   Let us also remember those among us who do not have a mother at home.
   May God compensate them in other ways.

NOTES – MOTHERING SUNDAY

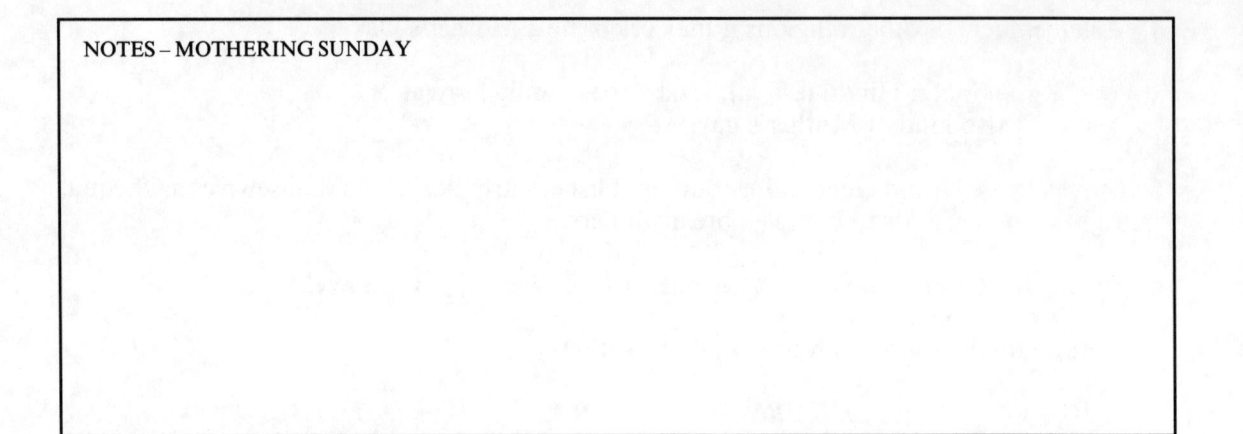

CONCENTRATION

1. The world is full of noise. Rarely, if ever, is there complete silence:

    – fridge humming
    – aeroplane overhead
    – car passing
    – motorbike roaring
    – music centre blaring, etc.

2. Some people say they are frightened of silence.
   Makes them think too much about themselves and life.

3. Others long for bit of peace and quiet.
   Unfortunately, periods of silence usually interrupted.

4. Perhaps only places where still periods of quiet are places of worship.

    (Used to be true of libraries. Now librarians complain of hassle and stress of job).

5. Problem of all this noise is: difficulty in concentration.

6. Youngsters often claim: need background noise: eg TV, radio, records.

   But, can you concentrate fully with that distraction?

7. Many students claim they can. In fact, say it helps them to concentrate better.

8. You must decide that for yourself.

   However, fact is too many school reports say:
      'Lacks concentration'.

9. Often noticeable difference between supervised school work and homework.

10 Span of concentration for everybody, even at best, is limited.
    But this span for many seems recently to have diminished.
    TV advertisers said to work now on units of 10 secs concentration.

11 Increasingly, students: cannot sit still
                             daydream
                               lose interest.

12 What can you do to help concentration at home? A great deal:

    (a) Choose a quiet place to work.
        (Does school provide quiet room for some after school?)
    (b) Choose time when you are not too tired.
    (c) Set time limits.
        (Proved you learn more quickly with breaks. Actually continue to learn whilst resting).
    (d) Whilst working give it full attention.

13 Never be tempted to say 'I can't, I'm different'.

14 It needs:

          – self-discipline
          – organisation
          – forward planning

15 Concentration and meditation basis of many religions, particularly Buddhism.
    Takes time; needs to be worked at.
    BUT most rewarding.

PRAYER

In silence, Let us think about:

          – our attitude to study.
              (Pause)
          – how we can improve our concentration.
              (Pause)

      Let us resolve to exercise more self-discipline.

NOTES – CONCENTRATION

NATIONAL CHILDREN'S HOME

1. Thousands of children leave home these days and many finish up living rough.

   Huge, tragic social problem.

2. 100 years ago thousands of children (many very young) roaming streets of London: ragged, shoeless, filthy, hungry, wild.

3. Stole to get food or employed by 'Fagins'. (Dickens: 'Oliver Twist').

4. Methodist Minister, Rev. Thomas Bowman Stephenson decided to do something about it.

   Opened small Home for Destitute Children in Lambeth on 7 July 1869.

5. Work did not stop there.

   Did not want large institutions so opened Family Homes in small houses.

6. Grew into wide-ranging organisation known as:

   National Children's Home.

7. Today has 200 centres and many teams of child care workers who look after 16,000 children and young people annually.

8. NCH works increasingly in community context.

   Activities include:
   - homeplay projects
   - family centres
   - befriending services
   - work with young offenders

   as well as traditional residential care

9. Also NCH Careline (telephone counselling service) set up 10 years ago.

10. NCH states is responding to dangers that threaten:
    - neglect
    - violence
    - unemployment
    - drugs/alcohol
    - disability

- poverty
- crime
- family breakdown.

11　Child abuse figures published 1992 by Department of Health indicate:

over 39,000 children at risk in UK.

(Give details of any existing school support scheme for NCH or, if thought appropriate, suggest one be started).

PRAYER

Let us ask for God's blessing on all who care for children and young people in need, and especially for care workers with the National Children's Home.

```
NOTES – NATIONAL CHILDREN'S HOME
```

TOWN PLANNING

1　What do you think of the town you live in/or the nearest one?

2　Has it the facilities you require?
Is it:

- pleasant?
- clean?
- attractive?
- spacious?
- healthy?
- friendly?

If not, why not?

3　Trouble is most towns were not planned.

Biggest problems began with Industrial Revolution.
People flocked to towns where industry was beginning to flourish.

4　Bosses provided houses for mill and factory workers.

Many small, basic, back-to-back.
    (e.g. TV Coronation Street).

5 Some bosses more enlightened, e.g. Cadbury Bros.

Life had not been easy for the Cadburys.
Nearly became bankrupt.
Then installed new machine for making cocoa, from Holland.
This was great success and business took off.

6 Cadbury brothers cared for workers.

Built new factory,
but also provided new homes, shops, gardens, library, sports facilities and a meeting-house.

    (Cadburys belonged to Society of Friends – Quakers).

7 All this set in model village, Bournville, on outskirts of Birmingham.

Still largely same today. Has real community atmosphere.
Can be visited (including tour of chocolate factory!)

8 Been other attempts at 'model' communities. Not always so successful,

    e.g. Cumbernauld, near Glasgow, in Scotland.
    Built in 1956. Claimed to be safest town in Britain.
    Everything thought of: clean, safe, easily accessible.
    Multi-storey town centre.

9 BUT when residents interviewed on TV said:
    – concrete jungle
    – no heart
    – no neighbourliness.

10 Perhaps that's reason for TV adverts for new towns:
    'Come and live in . . . . . .'
Fact is, many people find such towns soulless.

11 Cadbury Bros. had right idea.

Village/town needs heart, soul.
However well planned, it's people who give sense of community.

12 Take example of slum clearance.

Replaced by high-rise flats. Now being knocked down. Why?
No neighbourliness, no sense of belonging, no community spirit.
Some even have sign on wall:

    NO BALL GAMES, NO CYCLING, NO SKATEBOARDING.

13 It's quality of life we must consider.

   This doesn't mean facilities don't matter. They do.
   But not most important.
   It's people who matter most and who need to contribute to community

14 Come back to original question:

   > What do you think of your town? (or nearest town?)

15 If you were planning new town,

   > What would you consider as essentials?
   > How could you give it a sense of community?

16 Perhaps you would like to think about it.

   If you wish, you could write down your thoughts with town plan and give it to me.
   (Could be made into competition with display of best).

   PRAYER:
   Help us to be active members of our community, taking care to safeguard and respect our local environment.

NOTES – TOWN PLANNING

HAVES AND HAVENOTS

1 In New Testament Jesus told parable of: Dives (Latin = Rich Man) and Lazarus – poor man.
   > (Read Luke 16 vv 19–31).

2 A parable is story with moral.

   (Schoolboy howler: Parable is heavenly story with no earthly meaning.)

3 Jesus's parables usually illustrated one main point.
   So, let's not pay too much attention to colourful background imagery of next world.
   Typical of story-telling of time.

4 Let's also disregard questions parable poses:

   – Is there second chance in after-life?

   – Would people be more likely to believe in after-life if someone returned from dead?

5 Main point of Jesus's parable is:

   Our conduct on this earth affects our destiny.
   ACT 1: (Visible world).
   Dives decked out in fine clothes and 'living it up'.
   Lazarus in rags with ulcers licked by street dogs.
   Living off bread used by rich man and guests to clean hands before throwing away.

   To sum up:
   Dives – luxury and finery.
   Lazarus – rags and sores.

   ACT 2: (Invisible world)
   Dramatic change in two men's fortunes:
   Lazarus in heaven enjoying banquet;
   Dives in hell, tongue parched, tormented by flames.
   Sees Lazarus for first time. Tries to make friends.
   But Father Abraham says: 'Too late. You had your chance.
   There is a great gulf fixed.'

   To sum up: God has made his judgment on the two lives.

6 What does parable have to say to us today?

   Some have suggested:
   We in West are Dives. Out there in Africa lies wretched Lazarus.

   Just as Dives sinned against Lazarus because, for want of caring, never put himself in poor man's place.
   So we are guilty if we do nothing about poverty and misery of others.

7 Poverty, famine, disease, death rampant in Third World.
   What can we do?

   (a) Give money to support:
   – Comic Relief
   – Save the Children Fund
   – Oxfam
   – Christian Aid, etc.

   (b) Offer time and service:
                (e.g. some spend time between school and college in voluntary service).
   (c) Campaign against waste: e.g.
          – butter mountains
          – milk lakes
          – crops destroyed because uneconomic to sell.
   (d) Discipline ourselves against over-indulgence.

8 Remember words of Jesus (Matt 25 v 45) – Good News Version:
    'I tell you, whenever you refused to help one of these least important ones, you refused to help me'.

PRAYER:

Through no merit of our own we have been born and brought up in an affluent society. Let us remember those who, through no fault of their own, have been born and brought up where poverty, famine and disease are the accepted norm.

```
NOTES – HAVES AND HAVENOTS



```

BLINDNESS

1 Biggest fear of many people is losing sight.
    Visual defects one of commonest causes of disability in world.

2 World Health Organisation (WHO) defines:

      profound blindness as
      'inability to count fingers at a distance of 10ft'.

      partial blindness as
      'inability to count fingers at a distance of 20ft or less'.

      Term: 'visual handicap' covers both.

3 In Britain:

        – nearly 1 million blind (1 in 60).
        – more than 20,000 children growing up with visual handicap.
        – 4 out of 5 visually handicapped people over retirement age.

– 1 in 5 over 75 blind or partially sighted.
– eye accidents at home result in 200 hospital admissions a day.

4   Registered blind or partially sighted may get special help eg disability benefit.

BUT some receive little or no help from State.
On average, blind people have 1/3rd less to live on than sighted people.

5   Visually handicapped are just like everyone else:
   EXCEPT that they cannot see properly, e.g.
   – go to school
   – get jobs
   – bring up families
   – enjoy holidays, friends, hobbies
   – AND WATCH TV.

(Following information is taken from official literature of Royal National Institute for Blind. Use as much or as little of it as you think fit. You could spread material over more than one assembly. An overhead projector would help.)

6   What can we do to help?
(Remember: Don't assume help is needed. Always ask first).
In conversation:

   – talk naturally
       (Don't be afraid to say: 'Nice to see you')
   – say who you are
   – before moving, say you are leaving.
In street:

   – help across street
       (Walk slightly in front with blind person holding arm)
   – help into car
       (Say which way car is facing. Place person's hand on car roof over open door)
   – always warn blind person if approaching slope or stairs
Indoors:

   – show round room and describe furniture
   – help visitor into chair
       (Put person's hand on arm or back of chair and they will find own way)
   – DON'T leave doors half open or things lying on floor
   – at mealtimes say what food is
   – DON'T fill cups or glasses to brim.

7   Royal National Institute for Blind (RNIB) provides over 50 different services eg:

   – schools and colleges
   – job training
   – life skills training
   – braille and talking books
   – old people's homes and holiday hotels.

Also supports research into prevention of blindness and campaigns for fairer deal for visually handicapped.

8 (If school does not support work of RNIB; A donation? An event?
Address is: 224, Great Portland Street, London, W1N6AA
TEL: 071-388-1266.

PRAYER:

Thank God for the wonderful gift of sight; for the ability to appreciate beautiful colours, to read books, watch films and television, to see our family and friends.
Bless the work of the RNIB and similar organisations.
May we do all *we* can to help the blind and partially sighted.

NOTES – BLINDNESS

WRITING ON THE WALL

1 May have heard expression:
'The writing's on the wall'.

2 No, it's not someone complaining about graffiti.
But, in passing, graffiti a problem.
Ball-point pens and spray cans wonderful inventions.
However, misused, can result in disfigurement of school and environment.

3 Expression 'writing on wall' has quite different meaning.
Origin (though not actual words) found in Bible. (Daniel chap 5).

Story of Belshazzar's Feast:

One night King Belshazzar, King of Babylon, invited 1000 noblemen to great banquet.
He ordered gold and silver cups and bowls which his father, King Nebuchadnezzar, had stolen from Temple in

Jerusalem should be brought in.
All drank wine from them and praised gods made of gold,
silver, bronze, iron, wood and stone.
Suddenly human hand appeared and began writing on plaster
wall.
King saw hand as it was writing and was terrified.
Brought in magicians, wizards and astrologers to read
writing but no-one could.
Mother remembered man in kingdom who was wise and had
'spirit of gods in him'. Name was Daniel.
Was brought to king and told would be 3rd in kingdom if
he could interpret writing.
Said did not desire gifts but nevertheless would read
writing.
Daniel told king he had not learned lessons from father
whom God removed from throne for cruelty, stubbornness
and worship of idols.
Told him he was also arrogant, bringing in cups and bowls
stolen from Temple and praising idols
So this is what God had written on wall:
    'Mene, mene, tekel, upharsin.'
  (Number, number, weight, division.)
NUMBER: God has numbered days of your kingdom and brought it to an end.

WEIGHT: You have been weighed in scales and found to be too light.

DIVISIONS: Your kingdom is divided up and given to Medes and Persians.

4. Very dramatic story.
   Made into film.
   Subject of wonderful choral work by William Walton.

5. It's middle of message on wall we use as warning:
   'You have been weighed in scales and found to be too light' or, in older version:
   ('You have been weighed in balances and found wanting')

6. Sign of coming disaster.
   Warning we're not up to scratch.

7. Perhaps in school would be applicable to progress towards exams, particularly public exams.

   Mock exam can show us we've been weighed on scales and found to be too light.

8. End of Belshazzar's story is very sad:

   that night there was a coup, Belshazzar was assassinated and Darius, the Mede, seized power.

9. For us, fate not inevitable.

When 'writing appears on wall' we can take notice.
Change ways. Turn over new leaf. Act in time and begin to work.

10. Hope we shan't have to say to any of you;

   'the writing's on the wall'.
   But if we do, your fate will be in own hands.

   PRAYER:
   Make us ever conscious of our own shortcomings.
   Teach us not to be stubborn and arrogant but rather to be humble and self-critical.

NOTES – WRITING ON THE WALL

TALENTS

1. Jesus tells story of Talents, (Matt 25 vv 14–16)

   (Read version of story which retains word 'talent' rather than 'coin'.)

2. 'Talent' in N. T. times was unit of coinage. Worth lot of money.
   When you or I speak of talent we use it to mean 'natural gift'.

3. What Jesus is saying about investing money applies equally to natural talent:

   If you don't use it, you will lose it.

4. Often, as in story, people with greatest talents feel confident and adventurous.
   Can afford to be bold, using and improving their many talents.
   Can even choose which talent to exploit.

5. Not so for persons with only one talent.
   Know they must succeed with this one or not succeed at all.

6. Fact is only few have number of talents. The exception.
   Majority of us have only one talent.

Needs to be used, invested, allowed to grow.
Certainly we should never bury our talent.
And there is nobody, REPEAT NOBODY, who has no talents at all.

7 Story of prisoner of war in German POW Camp in last war.
Like rest, received parcels with bars of chocolate.
Didn't eat them but stored them up for end of war.
When finally liberated, found parcel heap of uneatable mould.

8 To have even one talent is something to be proud of.

Remember, if you don't use it you will lose it.

PRAYER:

Teach us to understand that talents kept to ourselves are wasted, but those shared bring happiness to ourselves and joy to others.

NOTES – TALENTS

COMMUNITY RESPONSIBILITY

1 An old tale from India:

> Four foolish beggars met by chance in beggars' hut.
> Been begging all day, holding out bowls.
> At sunset limped to hut, sat round fire.
> Discontented and suspicious.
> First beggar had nothing in bowl except little meat.
> Second beggar – bowl half filled with vegetables
> Third beggar – only few spices.
> Fourth beggar – few handfuls of rice.

2 Talked and grumbled. Then one suggested if put water in pot over fire and each threw in contents of bowl, would be broth for all.

3   Pot filled with water and beggars sat round eagerly.
    1st beggar – thinking he was clever – realised if others threw in spices, vegetables and rice, could keep meat to himself.
    So pretended to throw in meat.
    2nd beggar thought same – pretended to throw in vegetables.
    3rd beggar likewise with spices and 4th with rice.
    All hid food under rags.

4   No end of quarrelling when pot finally lifted from fire and *nothing* found in water.

5   Often said: 'You get out of life what you put into it'.

    And it's true. Put nothing in and you get nothing out.

6   So true of life at school.

    Those who take every benefit – use all facilities, resources, expertise without thought of what contribution they could make.

7   Success of school community depends on everybody playing part.

    Giving something back.
    Thinking of common good.

8   Community outside is same.

    At best when everyone plays active role, contributing, doing one's bit.

9   Unfortunately, always few parasites on any living organism.
    Can sustain few, but if too many, life sucked out.

10 If you haven't done so before, think about what you can do to make this school a better place for us all.

    PRAYER:

    Let us not sit back and wait for others to carry out the responsibilities of community life. Make us willing contributors to the common good.

NOTES – COMMUNITY RESPONSIBILITY

APRIL

1. No-one certain how April got its name.

   In old days month of April was called Avril (as in French)
   Romans called it Aprilis, (possibly from Latin verb 'aperire' = to open.)
   Represents opening of new season of growth and fertility.

2. April famous for its showers. Saying:

   > March winds and April showers
   > Bring forth May flowers.

3. Poet Robert Browning (1812–1889). Lived in sunny Italy.
   Longed to be back in England. Wrote:

   > Oh to be in England
   > Now that April's there,
   > And whoever wakes in England
   > Sees, some morning, unawares,
   > That the lowest boughs and the brushwood sheaf
   > Round the elm tree bole are in tiny leaf
   > While the chaffinch sings on the orchard bough
   > In England now.

4. April is also important for Sikhs.

   Celebration of Baisakhi. Sikh New Year.
   Usually falls on 13th (sometimes 14th).
   On this date in 1699 last Guru, Gobind Singh, chose first five disciples – The 'Khalsa' or 'Pure Ones'.

5. 23rd April very important.

   Two anniversaries:
   > Feast of St George, Patron Saint of England.
   > Birthday of William Shakespeare.

6. St George became Patron Saint in reign of Edward III when Order of Garter was founded.
   Little known about life.
   Said to have been Christian who became Roman soldier.
   Emperor Diocletian hated Christians. Hunted them down and put to death.
   George himself, in fact, chose to die rather than give up Christian faith.
   Executed 23rd April 303.
   His flag, red cross on white background, emblem of Crusaders riding into battle, became flag of England.
   Now Red Cross forms part of Union Jack.

7 William Shakespeare.
   Throughout world recognised as one of greatest playwrights.
   Known as 'Bard (Poet/Singer in Celtic language) of Avon'.
   Born Stratford-upon-Avon in 1564.
   Greatest period between 1600 and 1607 when produced:
       e.g. Comedies – 'As You Like It' and 'Twelfth Night'.
           Tragedies – 'Hamlet', 'Othello', 'King Lear' and 'Macbeth'.
   Sonnets date from 1609.
   Died in 1616.
   Annual Shakespeare Festival when plays performed in Shakespeare Memorial Theatre in Stratford.

PRAYER:

Let us pause for a moment and in silence remember the significant contributions of famous people of past.
In particular (today) let us remember St George and William Shakespeare.

NOTES – APRIL

AMNESTY INTERNATIONAL

1 Imagine you return home this evening.
   Knock on door. Your father answers it.
   After some time father does not return so you go to door.
   You see father being bundled into car by four men.
   What would you do?

2 You would probably call police who would start search for father.

3 This story, taken from Amnesty International publicity, based on incident in Chile.
   Daughter could not call police because it was police who took father away.
   Police denied all knowledge.
   Never saw father again.

4   Similar stories all round world.
    People imprisoned for beliefs, in countries like S Korea and Peru.
    People tortured in China, Pakistan and Turkey.
    Thousands waiting to die on Death Row in USA, Jamaica and Japan.

5   In Spring 1961 lawyer, Peter Benenson, travelling on bus in Central London, reading newspaper.
    Read story of two students having drink in cafe in Lisbon.
    Raised glasses and toasted 'Liberty'.
    For this arrested and imprisoned.

6   Peter got off bus, went into nearby church to think.
    Decided to write newspaper article about students and many other thousands of 'prisoners of conscience'.

7   Article published in Observer 28th May 1961, entitled:
            'The Forgotten Prisoners'.
    Called on people everywhere to work impartially and peacefully for their release.

8   In response, over 1000 offers of support for idea of international campaign for human rights.
    Began as one-year campaign called 'Appeal for Amnesty'.
    Led to birth of Amnesty International.

9   Over last 30 years or so, worked on behalf of more than 42,000 cases. Of these, over 39,000 have been closed.

10 Now more than 1 million human rights activists in 70 or so countries.

11 Need still very great:

            – 80 countries have prisoners of conscience
            – 15 countries detain political prisoners without charge or trial
            – 100 countries torture prisoners
            – 92 countries continue to use death penalty.

12 Peter Benenson did something about it.
    What can you do?

            – Youth Action Group Affiliation costs £18 per annum (1993)
              (Amnesty International, British Section, 91–119 Roseberry Avenue
              London, EC1 4RE.)
            – Contact local Amnesty group
                    (List sent on affiliation)
            – Write letters to Heads of State e.g. countries already mentioned
            – Arrange event in aid of Amnesty International.

THOUGHT FOR DAY
(A Litany for the Day of Human Rights – Salvador de Madariaga).

For those who grasp their prison bars helplessly
   so that we may walk free – a thought.
For those who rot in the dark
   so that we may walk in the sun – a thought.
For those whose ribs have been broken
   so that we may breathe our fill – a thought.
For those whose faces have been slapped
   so that we may walk in fear of no hand – a thought.
For those whose mouths have been gagged
   so that we may speak out – a thought.
For those whose wives live in anguish
   so that our wives may live happy – a thought.
For those whose country is in chains
   so that our country may be free – a thought.
And for the jailers and for their torturers – a thought.
   The saddest of all, they are the most maimed,
   and the day of reckoning is bound to come.

NOTES – AMNESTY INTERNATIONAL

PEACE-KEEPING

1. Despite all progress in education and civilisation, end of Cold War and work of UN, war still continues all over world.

2. Constant dream is lasting peace.

   But is it possible?

3. Some say war inevitable.

   Humans are greedy, violent, selfish.
   Nations only interested in own economic, ethnic and political survival.

4. Few people dedicated pacifists: e.g. in this country, Lord Soper, Tony Benn, MP. (Use own examples).

   Lord Soper has always believed war is wrong.
   Now thinks wars no longer practicable.

Admits may be short-term situation in which you have to fight, but says:

> 'That's like one clip in a film: it means little by itself. You have to make a non-violent script.
> What's morally wrong becomes inoperable. War turns in on itself.'

5   In 1914 and 1939 wars Britain allowed conscripts to object to military service on grounds of conscience.

Conscientious objectors, or 'conscies', as they were nicknamed, went before judge and tribunal to state case.

6   One favourite question was:

> 'What would do if you saw enemy soldier attacking your mother?'

This brings it right down to personal level and highlights terrible dilemma for those believing in non-violence.

7   Conscientious objectors suffered greatly in 1914–1918 war.

People showed them white feather, spat on them, wrote abusive letters and broke windows of homes.

8   Despite all difficulties, some people still believe pacifism is only answer.

9   Trying to make peace and keep peace important ways of attempting to lessen horrible consequences of war.

10   UN has peace-keeping role.

Operations fall into two categories:
- observer missions (eg monitoring of cease-fire agreements)
- peace-keeping forces (eg maintaining buffer zones between hostile forces.)

11   UN peace-keepers authorised to use force only in self-defence.

Strongest support is international community.
But recently had to engage in armed conflict to stop unlawful aggression.

12   Annual cost to UN estimated April 1993 – 2.7 billion US dollars.

13   Some think UN too weak, 'toothless'. Often ignored e.g. Bosnia.

Is there any other answer?
Surely any attempt to make peace must be good.
Remember comment of Sir Winston Churchill:

> 'Jaw, jaw is better than war, war.'

MEDITATION
(Poem by Matti Yosef, 9 years).

   I don't like wars
They end up with monuments;
I don't want battles to roar
Even in neighbouring continents.

I like Spring
Flowers producing,
Fields covered with green,
The wind in the hills whistling.

Drops of dew I love,
The scent of jasmine as night cools,
Stars in darkness above,
And rain singing in pools.

I don't like wars. They end
In wreaths and monuments;
I like Peace come to stay
And it will some day.

NOTES – PEACE-KEEPING

DANCING

1. Dancing always been one of human activities.
   When happy, people have danced.
   Also found pleasure in watching others dance.

2. Each tribe, race, group of people developed own particular forms of dancing.
   These can still be seen in tribal and national celebrations.

3. In England Morris Dancing has been tradition and dancing round Maypole.
   Associated with death of winter and birth of spring.

4. In Queen Elizabeth I's reign danced in pairs.
   In 19th century ballroom dancing introduced.
   Since then rock'n'roll, twisting, shaking, break dancing, rap, etc.

5   Scots perform Highland Fling, sword dances and reels.
Irish famous for jig.
Americans for square dancing.
Russians have boisterous dances whilst Indians perform delicate, graceful body movements.

6   From earliest times dancing formed part of religious celebrations.

One of the oldest ways of asking help from gods.
Dancing represented what wanted gods to do by miming:
      e.g. falling of rain
          growing of crops
          sunshine
          death of enemies.

7   In India dance and drama are used to represent stories of Hindu gods and goddesses. Dancing popular at Diwali (Hindu New Year – Festival of Lights, and at Ratri celebrating god Shiva, called 'Lord of the Dance'.

8   King David in O.T. astonished people of Israel with dance of celebration to God for victory over enemies (2 Sam 6 v 14)

9   Sydney Carter wrote song about the Lord of the Dance.
He was thinking of Jesus as the one who danced.

        (Read poem or assembly to sing)

        Dance then, wherever you may be,
        I am the Lord of the Dance, said he,
        And I'll lead you all, wherever you may be,
        And I'll lead you all in the dance, said he.

        I danced in the morning
        When the world was begun,
        And I danced in the moon
        And the stars and the sun;
        And I came down from heaven
        And I danced on the earth,
        At Bethlehem I had my birth.

        I danced on the Sabbath
        And I cured the lame;
        The holy people
        Said it was a shame.
        They whipped and they stripped
        And they hung me on high,
        And left me there
        On a Cross to die.

        They cut me down
        And I leapt up high;

I am the life
That'll never, never die.
I'll live in you
If you'll live in me;
I am the Lord
Of the Dance, said he.

Dance then, wherever you may be,
I am the Lord of the Dance, said he,
And I'll lead you all, wherever you may be,
And I'll lead you all in the Dance, said he.

10 (Conclude with):
Dancing is sign that life carries on.
(Then repeat):
Dance, then, wherever you may be,
I am the Lord of the Dance, said he,
And I'll lead you all, wherever you may be,
And I'll lead you all in the Dance, said he.

NOTES – DANCING

ATTENTION TO DETAIL

1 There's well-known proverb:

Look after pence and pounds will look after themselves.

Refers literally to attitude to money.
Easy to fritter away small amounts – penny here, 20p there.
Not uncommon to find 1p coin lying on ground. Nobody bothered to pick it up.

2 Many self-made millionaires, however, claim made fortune by looking after small sums of money.

3 Proverb also points to important principle in life:

take care over small things; pay attention to detail.

4 Story of how Jacques Lafitte became famous banker.

> Son of poor carpenter in Bayonne, France.
> Decided to seek fortune. Arrived in Paris without references, qualifications or influential friends.
> Diligently sought employment over days and weeks but unsuccessful.
> One morning applied for job at office of famous Swiss banker, M. Perregaux.
> By chance, M. Perregaux himself interviewed him.
> After few questions, shook head, no vacancy at moment.
> Jacques left bank, walked slowly across courtyard.
> As he did so, stooped down picked something up, and sauntered into street.
> Suddenly tapped on shoulder by man who said:
> 'Excuse me, sir. I'm attendant at Bank. M. Perregaux wishes to see you again'.
> Jacques returned to face great man.
> 'I saw you stoop down and pick up something', said M. Perregaux.
> 'What was it?'
> 'Only this,' said Jacques, taking bright new pin out of lapel.
> 'Ah!' said M. Perregaux, 'that changes everything. We always have a vacancy for someone who is careful about little things. You may start at once.'
> Ultimately, Jacques Lafitte assumed complete control of what later became Perregaux, Lafitte et Cie (Compagnie).

5 American statesman, scientist and writer, Benjamin Franklin (1706–1790) wrote:

> A little neglect may breed mischief
> . . . for want of a nail the shoe was lost;
>   for want of a shoe the horse was lost;
>   for want of a horse the rider was lost.
>
> Someone later added;
>   for want of a rider the battle was lost.

6 Jesus sums it up in Luke 16 v 10/11:

> Someone who can't be trusted in things that don't matter, can't be trusted in things that really matter.

PRAYER:

Experience has shown that great things can develop from very small beginnings.
Make us diligent, conscientious, paying attention to detail, so that we may prove ourselves worthy of other people's trust and confidence.

NOTES – ATTENTION TO DETAIL

SINCERITY

1. Difficult to know if someone is being sincere.

    Often regarded as joke when people say:
    > 'And I mean that most sincerely!'

2. Puts doubt in mind just as when people say:

    > 'No, honestly, cross my heart!'

3. We finish friendly, social letters with words:

    > Yours sincerely,

    Become recognised form of ending for letter addressed to person by name, eg Dear John/Jean.
    (As opposed to formal letters beginning with:
    > 'Dear Sir/Madam which finish with:
    > 'Yours faithfully').

4. Have you ever wondered what 'Yours sincerely' really means?
    Has been suggested (not proved) that word 'sincerity' goes back to potters of ancient Rome.
    There were, of course, good and bad potters.
    Bad made cracked vessels look good.
    Did this by filling cracks with wax so that customers in market would never notice.
    However, when poured hot water in, wax melted. Discovered they'd been cheated.
    Good potters scorned use of wax and broke cracked pots.

    So good potters would put out sign saying: 'SINE CERA' – without wax.
    In other words, were sound, genuine, reliable.

5. So that's what we're saying when we write 'Yours sincerely'.
    I'm genuine, honest, reliable. You can trust me.
    In other words I'm precisely what I seem.
    Not hyprocite, pretender.

6. Sincerity is rare and valuable commodity in world where people are so ready to pretend, cheat, give false impression.
    There are even professional confidence tricksters.

    PRAYER

    Guard us against falsehood and hypocrisy.
    Give us the desire to be sincere in all we say and do, so that others may be able to depend on us and trust our word.

NOTES – SINCERITY

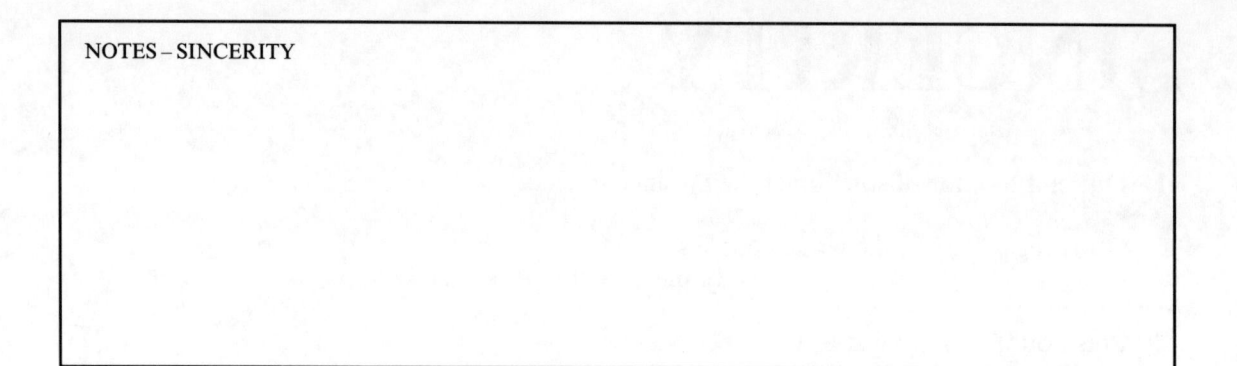

PATIENCE

1 There is saying;

> 'Patience is a virtue, possess it if you can.'

(Next line can be controversial):

> 'Often found in woman, never found in man!'

2 That is sexual stereotyping.

Plenty of **men** patient. Plenty of **women** impatient.

3 Whether male or female, all need at times to have patience.

Things don't always happen overnight.
Can take time for things to develop and mature.

4 Of course, there are times for instant action – emergencies occur:

> e.g. fire
> snatching child from middle of road
> buying bargain in sale.

5 However, patience can sometimes win where force and aggression fail.

La Fontaine, 17th century poet, famous for his fables.
One is about lion and rat.

> Rat ran between lion's paws and he let it go.
> Little later, lion got caught in net. Despite all roaring and rage could do nothing to help himself.
> Rat, on other hand, very patiently gnawed away at mesh until there was big enough hole for lion to escape.

6 Aesop, Greek fable-writer (6th century BC) told story of crow, ready to die of thirst, found jug with water in it.

> But water in jug so low couldn't reach it.
> Tried overturning it, breaking it, but was not strong enough.
> Seeing some pebbles nearby, thought of plan.
> Dropped them in, one by one.
> Gradually water rose until nearly reached brim.
> Patient bird at last able to quench thirst.

7 A 17th century French writer once made very interesting comment;
'Genius is only a great aptitude for patience'.

8 Certainly, many great inventions, discoveries and scientific advances have only been achieved by tremendous patience and perseverance.

9 St Paul in one of his letters in New Testament, likened life to race and suggested. like distance runners who bide their time, we should run with patience the race that is set before us.

PRAYER;
(By Reinhold Niebuhr, 1892–1971)

Give us, Lord,
The courage to change those things that can be changed,
The patience to bear those things that cannot be changed,
And the wisdom to know the difference.

NOTES – PATIENCE

HARVEST OF THE SEA

1 Normally when we celebrate harvest think of harvest of land.
In many parts of world means harvest of grain: wheat, barley, etc.

2 But there is another important harvest that goes on all time:

Harvest of Sea.

3 Often fraught with danger:

> gales
> mountainous seas
> dangerous rocks.

4 Nowadays, fishing even more difficult:

> – poisoned waters – e.g. oil spillage from super tankers
> – limits imposed on periods and quantities of catches
> – unfair competition e.g. Russian and other factory ships which gather up all fish, even smallest, thus depleting fish stocks in seas.

5 Fish is still relatively inexpensive and considered important ingredient in healthy diet.

6 Do not always appreciate courage and determination of fishermen who risk lives to bring fish to our tables.

7 No doubt fishermen have cause, from time to time, to be thankful for services of Royal National Lifeboat Institution.

8 Voluntary organisation. No government money.

Dependent on gifts, donations and flag days.
Started by Sir William Hillary. Lived in Douglas, Isle of Man.
Could see huge seas from window.
Became member of local lifeboat crew and helped rescue many people.

9 Saw need for national organisation, responsible for all lifeboats.

Published idea in 1823. Body formed in 1824.
Received Royal Charter in 1854.

10 Members of lifeboat crews give service freely.

Thousands of lives saved through their skill and courage.

11 On one hand something quite marvellous about sea.

Psalmist in O.T. says:
> 'They that go down to the sea in ships and occupy their business in great waters . . . see the works of the Lord and His wonders in the deep'.

12 On other hand, Psalmist reminds us (Psalm 46):
> 'God is our shelter and strength,
>   always ready to help in times of trouble.
>   So we will not be afraid. . . .
>   even if the seas roar and rage.'

PRAYER

(Could be sung as hymn).
Eternal Father, strong to save,
Whose arm doth bind the restless wave,
Who bidd'st the mighty ocean deep
Its own appointed limits keep:
> *O hear us when we cry to thee*
> *For those in peril on the sea.*

NOTES – HARVEST OF THE SEA

DEATH OF MEMBER OF SCHOOL

(Assembly will need to be adapted according to whether for student or member of staff/governor, etc).

1. *Opening Remarks:*
   I am sure we all felt saddened/shocked to hear of the death of . . .
   At times like these it is very difficult to think of anything to say which would be appropriate. Words fail us.
   So let us use this assembly to express our sorrow and remember with gratitude the life of . . .

2. *Either* sing the hymn: 'The Lord's my shepherd',
   Or read: Psalm 23.

3. What we *can* do is show kindness and friendship to those who mourn, and offer our sympathy and condolences to:
   parent/s   )
   wife/husband   )
   brothers/sisters   )   as appropriate
   colleagues   )
   friends   )

4 *A Short Tribute from member of staff and/or governor and/or student, as appropriate.*

5 *If Departed is Christian*: Read Revelations 21 vv1–5.
If not: Read from relevant Holy Book
Or: Read this extract from 'The Prophet' by Kahlil Gibran:
(Can also be used in addition to Christian or other reading).

> Then Almitra spoke, saying, We would ask now of Death.
> And he said:
> You would know the secret of death.
> But how shall you find it unless you seek it in the heart of life?
> The owl whose night-bound eyes are blind unto the day cannot unveil the mystery of light.
> If you would indeed behold the spirit of death, open your heart wide unto the body of life.
> For life and death are one, even as the river and the sea are one.
>
> In the depth of your hopes and desires lies your silent knowledge of the beyond;
> And like seeds dreaming beneath the snow your heart dreams of spring.
> Trust the dreams, for in them is hidden the gate to eternity.
> Your fear of death is but the trembling of the shepherd when he stands before the king whose hand is to be laid on him in honour.

6 Let us stand in silence in memory of. . . . (1 or 2 mins)

7 *Conclude with:*
Either Christian prayer:
Almighty God, Father of all mercies and giver of all comfort, look with kindness on those of us who mourn.
Be with us in our sadness and loss and strengthen our trust in you, Through Jesus Christ our Lord.

> *Or:* 'All is Well', (After an original by Canon Henry Scott Holland of St. Paul's Cathedral)

Death is nothing at all.
I have only slipped away into the next room.
I am I and you are you.
Whatever we were to each other,
That we still are.

NOTES – DEATH OF MEMBER OF SCHOOL

SENIOR STUDENT ASSEMBLIES

MORALITY

1. 1988 Education Act states:

    'A balanced and broadly based curriculum which promotes the spiritual, moral, cultural, mental and physical development of pupils at the school and of society.'

2. Schools have obligation to help **spiritual** and **moral** development of students: first two in list.

3. 'And of society' – strange phrase. How can schools promote moral development of society?

    Perhaps it is by giving students moral foundation?

4. Could argue: Everybody responsible for restoration of morality in society.

5. Archbishop of Canterbury, Rev Dr George Carey, on a Remembrance Sunday said:

    'I am profoundly concerned about the steady moral drift of our society. Many seem to regard morals as a matter of individual opinion. We often hear people say: 'What I do in my private life is my business and nobody else's.'

6. Archbishop Carey would argue there is an absolute standard of morality. Is he right?

7. Certainly there have to be shared values. These bind society together.

8. There are basic rules such as:

    'Do not murder, do not steal.'

    Though sometimes people argue about these.

9. Is it murder to carry out abortion or euthanasia?
    Is killing in war murder?

10. A man who was trained as a safe-breaker to steal Nazi documents during World War Two was imprisoned after war for doing same thing in civilian life.

11. Different standards of right and wrong.
    BUT cannot just live to ourselves. Live with others in society.
    Must respect other people and their property.

12. Trust is basic to life in a community-school or society outside.

13. We need to trust our national leaders – politicians, judges, etc.

Does it matter what they do in their private lives?
(Perhaps some students might like to debate this in a later assembly).

14 To trust, need shared values.

15 If believe in God, there is definition of 'right' and 'wrong'.

16 Many people today no longer believe in religion – or science, come to that.

   Big vacuum in which need to place your own set of values and principles.

17 School's task is to help you to do that.

   PRAYER

   We ask that we may all understand the need for personal principles and values.
   May what we do not only satisfy our own consciences but also cause no harm to others.

NOTES – MORALITY

DETERMINATION

1 Quite common for parents to say to children:
   'There's no such word as *can't*'.

2 Not always true. Some things impossible:
   e.g. to be in two places at once.
   (Though sometimes expected to be).

3 What people mean by 'No such thing as can't' is often lack of willpower that makes something seem impossible.

4   Perhaps it's 'won't' rather than 'can't'.

5   Until 1954 thought impossible to run sub-four-minute mile.
    But in May 1954 Roger Bannister broke four-minute barrier:

    He ran the first lap in 57.5 secs. and the half mile in 1 min. 58 secs.

6   In his book; *The Four-minute Mile* this is how he describes the last part of the race:

    'At three-quarters of a mile the effort was still barely perceptible; the time was 3 min. 0.7 seconds, and by now the crowd was roaring. Somehow I had to run the last lap in 59 seconds. Chataway led round the next bend and then I pounced, passed him at the beginning of the back straight, three hundred yards from the finish.

    I had a moment of mixed joy and anguish, when my mind took over. It was well ahead of my body and drew my body compellingly forward. I felt that the moment of a lifetime had come. There was no pain; only a great unity of movement and aim. The world seemed to stand still, or did not exist. The only reality was the next two hundred yards of track under my feet. The tape meant finality – extinction perhaps . . . I had now turned the last bend and there were only fifty yards more.

    My body had long since exhausted all its energy, but it went on running just the same. The physical overdraft came from greater will-power. This was the crucial moment when my legs were strong enough to carry me over the last few yards as they could never have done in previous years. With five yards to go the tape seemed almost to recede. Would I ever reach it? . . . I leapt at the tape like a man taking his last spring to save himself from the chasm that threatens to engulf him.

    My effort was over and I collapsed almost unconscious, with an arm on either side of me. It was only then that real pain overtook me. I felt like an exploded flashlight with no will to live; I just went on existing in the most passive physical state without being quite unconscious. Blood surged from my muscles and seemed to fell me. It was as if all my limbs were caught in an ever-tightening vice. I knew that I had done it before I even heard the time. I was too close to have failed, unless my legs had played strange tricks at the finish by slowing me down and not telling my tiring brain that they had done so.

    The stop-watches held the answer. The announcement came – 'Result of one mile . . . time, 3 minutes' – the rest lost in the roar of excitement. I grabbed Brasher and Chattway, and together we scampered round the track in a burst of spontaneous joy. We had done it – the three of us!

7   'Greater will-power'. Often this is what we need.
    Can make all the difference between failure and success.

8   Religious people believe God gives extra strength and power to human lives.

    All religions have examples of those who have achieved what seemed impossible with the help of God.

9 Jesus said: 'With God all things are possible'.

10 However, whether religious or not, let us never underestimate the strength of will-power.

PRAYER

May we this day run with patience the race that is set before us, growing in strength of will and steadfastness of character.

NOTES – DETERMINATION

FRIENDSHIP

1 By nature we humans are social beings.

Like being with other people.
Not all the time: sometimes prefer to be on own; only having to please ourselves.

2 A few people called 'loners'.

Seem to prefer own company most of time.
Or is it they can't relate? If so, that's quite a problem.

3 We all need friends. Better still, perhaps, one good friend we can really trust.

Rudyard Kipling wrote poem, 'The Thousandth Man'.*
    (*Explain 'man' represents men and women).
Theme is: a true friend stands by you through thick and thin.
Here is the first verse.
    (You may think it appropriate to read whole poem).

THE THOUSANDTH MAN

One man in a thousand, Solomon says,
Will stick more close than a brother.
And it's worth while seeking half your days
If you find him before the other.
Nine hundred and ninety-nine depend
On what the world sees in you,
But the Thousandth Man will stand your friend
With the whole round world agin you.

4   Expression: 'stick more close than a brother' Kipling uses, comes from Book of Proverbs in OT. Written by Solomon, son of King David. Hence in first line of poem: 'Solomon says'.
Actual quotation reads:

> 'A man who has friends must himself be friendly
> But there is a friend who sticks closer than a brother'.

5   Notice it says: 'must himself (herself) be friendly'.

Often secret of friendship.
Requires both give and take.
Many friendships break down because one-sided.

6   Some friendships do not last.

Not everyone can be relied on.
Friends, in fact, sorted out when times are difficult.
One of truest sayings is:

> 'A friend in need is a friend indeed'.

7   Common experience to find all your friends deserting you when you're going through really bad time.

Richard Barnfield sums this up in his poem:

EVERY FRIEND THAT FLATTERS THEE

> Every friend that flatters thee
> Is no friend in misery.
> Words are easy like the wind;
> Faithful friends are hard to find.
> Every man will be your friend
> Whilst thou hast wherewith to spend:

    But if score of crowns be scant,
    No man will supply thy want.

    He that is your friend indeed,
    He will help thee in thy need.
    If thou sorrow, he will weep;
    If thou wake, he cannot sleep;
    Thus of every grief in heart
    He with thee will bear a part.
    These are certain things to show
    Faithful friend from faltering foe.

8 In Bible is account of very close friendship, between David and Saul's son, Jonathan.

    Bible says: 'The soul of Jonathan was knit to the soul of David'.
    Wonderful way of expressing true friendship.

9 Friendships can survive our falling in love, marriage, having a family etc.

    In fact, best friendships last lifetime.

PRAYER:

Help us to appreciate that friendship requires both give and take. May we always be loyal and dependable so that others will feel confident to trust us with their friendship.

NOTES – FRIENDSHIP

VANITY, VANITY

1 May sometimes hear older people say to someone who's showing off:

    'Vanity, Vanity, All is Vanity'.
    Actually quotation from Bible. Comes from Book of Ecclesiastes in the O.T.
    Alternative title – The Preacher.

Full quotation –

'Vanity, Vanity, all is Vanity,' says the preacher.

2 Vanity something we frown on.
   Pride one of Seven Deadly Sins.
   Nothing worse than being called 'Big 'Ead.'

3 Yet need for pride in ourselves.
   Not liking oneself makes young people very depressed.
   Not realising their talents;
   Wishing they were someone else;
   Always thinking other people brainier
                    better looking
                    more likeable.

4 Need balance between being too proud and
                         not proud enough.
                    being self-confident but
                    not arrogant.

5 David Kossoff, well-known actor and broadcaster wrote what he described as a sort of prayer book. Called it '*You Have a Minute, Lord?*'
   He is really just talking to God.

6 One of his prayers is called; 'Vanity, Vanity.'

[Perhaps a student could read this.]

      Did I once read somewhere, Lord
         – you have a minute? –
         That all is vanity?
   Charles Laughton said it in a movie, too,
         quoting someone, surely.
   It's too good a line for a screenwriter.
         'Vanity, vanity, all is vanity',
   A remarkable thought in every way.

   One of the Deadlies, am I right?
   If not, certainly frowned upon, agreed?
   'Be not puffed up' another quote, Lord?
         And no doubt lots of others.
         A person grows up with it.
   'Don't be vain', 'Thinks a lot of himself',
   'Bit of a peacock' – or the gentle: 'Big 'ead!'

   Now Lord – a minute more? – a thought
         It seems to me, the older I get,
   I see that vanity has its place in the
         pattern of things.

  Maybe it is part of your pattern of
  things that as we get older we *do see it*.
 I understand; I've admired the pattern before.

   Yes, it has a place, vanity.
  A great *spur* to a person, vanity is.
    It makes a man hold his stomach in,
    and walk tall, and wear a hairpiece,
    and dress a bit too young.
    And buy too many rounds,
    and never never miss a mirror.

  A great leveller, vanity is.
 It can happen to anyone, it can.
    It keeps women young (in a way),
    keeps them caring, if only for themselves.
    Hairdresser instead of lunch;
    dressmaker before anything.
    And never, *never* miss a mirror.

Well, Lord (a moment more, I'm nearly done),
  The problem, not a big one, is this.
   If vanity has a place, a time,
  a position in your Pattern of Things,
  Show me the right place? *The right time*?
If it's not altogether bad and can help a person,
   it would be nice to do it right.
After all, a person doesn't want to get disliked

7 There are times when we should be 'Blowing our own trumpet.'
 We can be too self-effacing.
 As David Kossoff says:

   'If it's not altogether bad and can help a person
    it would be nice to do it right.

8 In his prayer he asks God to show him the right place and the right time.

NOTES – VANITY, VANITY

THE ENVIRONMENT

1. Increasingly conscious of dangers of destruction of **our** planet.

2. Warnings by scientists and many environmental organisations, e.g. Friends of the Earth.

3. Dangers include:

    (a) Hole in the ozone layer:

    Caused mainly by CFCs (chloro-fluorocarbons) and other gases.
    (Ozone layer extends between 30,000ft and 150,000ft above earth. Filters out harmful ultra-violet rays from sun which can cause skin cancer).

    (b) Destruction of Rain Forests
    e.g. in Brazil – for paper production and cattle ranching to produce beefburgers for fast food chains in West.
    (c) Trees killed by Acid Rain – caused by industrial chemicals.
    (d) Pollution of rivers and seas killing fish and causing danger to health.
    (e) Wild life exterminated by hunting. Ever decreasing area for habitants.

    [Use information from Friends of Earth, Greenpeace, etc.]

4. Responsibility is on every individual.
   No good holding up hands in horror, saying; 'What can I do?'

5. It's got to begin somewhere. It must begin with you and me. Governments are doing too little, too late.

6. What can we do?

    e.g. (a) Join an environmental organisation.
    (Through the school?)
    (b) Stop buying sprays that use CFCs.
    (c) Use recycled paper, etc.
    (d) Do not buy non bio-degradable materials.
    (e) Lobby your local councillors and/or MP about issues [mention specific issues].

7. Above all take care with your own environment:

    e.g. litter
    graffiti
    proper use of parks
    preservation of trees
    (trees newly planted often broken or uprooted).

8   It can start with respect for school environment. Ensuring pleasant place to work to in.

[Perhaps suggest poster competition about care of environment.]

PRAYER

God gave us a lovely world to live in but humans through negligence and greed have spoiled it. May we contribute to the restoration of the beauty and health of this planet by being thoughtful and considerate for everything and everyone around us.

NOTES – THE ENVIRONMENT

VIOLENCE

1   Have you ever tried word association games?

Used sometimes by therapists to discover what is in people's minds.

2   To be effective you must say first thing that comes in the head.

3   Let's try it:

Fish_____	?	(e.g. Chips)
Bacon_____	?	(e.g. Eggs)
Boy_____	?	(e.g. Girl)
Brussels_____	?	(e.g. Sprouts EEC)
Northern Ireland_____	?	(e.g. Terrorism Violence)

(Interesting to see if response to Northern Ireland is:
'Terrorism' or 'Violence' or 'IRA'. If not, point out in recent exercise of word association most responded with 'Bombing', 'Shooting', etc.)

91

4   Violence of terrorist commonplace now in our society.
    Not just Northern Ireland – [Name other places].

5   Why do people bomb and shoot?
    Believe violence will make people give way to their demands.
    Often has opposite effect. Makes those attacked even more determined.

6   Terrorism is extreme form of violence found in us all.

7   Experiment in USA:
        Person strapped into chair with electrodes attached.
        Two people behind glass screen had control which they believed could increase or decrease current fed to person in chair.
        Two people became crazy with power: increased and increased current.
        Fortunately actually no current. Just simulation.

8   Frightening what people can do to one another.
    Before saying: I could never be like that, examine yourself.

9   Children become violent to get own way:
                Bite, kick, scratch.

10 Primitive humans attacked through fear.
    With civilisation and education expect something better:
                Reason, understanding; discussion.

11 People blame:
            unemployment
            poverty
            alcohol

    All possible factors; or are they excuses?
    Alcohol certainly takes away our rational control.

12 Reason for violence can be trivial e.g. 'he/she looked at me.'

13 What can we do?
    Must start process of education very young:
    First impact by parents
            e.g. Is home violent?
    Then school:
            attitudes
            action taken against violence

14 All of us need to recognise violence is just below surface.
            e.g. angry car-driver.

15 Most religions teach:
            violence is destructive
            violence produces violence.

16   Remember it takes much more courage to be non-violent than it does to be violent. There's always another way.

17   Until human beings learn futility of aggression, this world will continue to be a place of violence.

PRAYER

Let us consider in silence the words of Jesus in the Sermon on the Mount:

Happy are those who work for peace! God will call them his children.

NOTES – VIOLENCE

AGE OF TELEVISION

(This assembly needs to be prepared a week or two in advance)

1   Many people fulfilled by literature.
    Through it learn to understand own lives and those of other people by confronting certain moral dilemmas.

2   Now live in 'The Age of Television':
        Will TV completely replace literature and newspapers?
        Could reading become obsolete skill?
        Would it matter?

3   (Ask for two volunteers to watch during coming week/fortnight, selection of TV programmes to include:
        news bulletin,
        play/film/video*
        sitcom.)

                                                    *ideally of book already read.

4   Volunteers must be prepared to speak to assembly for about five minutes on such topics as:
    (a) From what you have seen to what extent can TV replace:
        – newspapers?
        – literature?
    (b) If seen play/film/video of book already read:

- What were differences?
- Did it keep faithfully to text?
- Did it improve story or not?
- Did it spoil/enhance book for you?

5. Books are great human heritage.
   Ability to read and write marks us off from other animals.
   No cinema/TV screen can so represent depth of insight and understanding gained from books.
   Sometimes directors change, reduce or add to original.
   Plot often changed to give happy ending.

6. Philosophy, religion, science best understood from books.

7. In final analysis reading gives enormous pleasure.
   Life would be unbearable for many if they couldn't read.

PRAYER:

We give thanks for all the pleasure we receive from books, TV, theatre and cinema and accept with gratitude that all can play a part in enriching our lives.

NOTES – AGE OF TELEVISION

CHRISTMAS

1. Seems to begin in shops earlier and earlier.

   'Jingle Bells' and 'Rudolph the Red-Nose Reindeer' in early November.

2. Christmas hijacked by commercial enterprise.

   Good winner, soft touch. 'Hyped' out of all recognition.

3. Think of expense of wrapping paper. All torn within minutes. Was it worth it?

4. Cards pour through letterbox, some from people you have forgotten to send to.

One public figure decided enough was enough. When he received Christmas cards, he simply wrote on them: 'And the same to you' and sent them back. They never sent any more.

5   That's very drastic. Most of us like receiving Christmas cards. Trouble is it gets out of hand.

6   Many people seem nicer at Christmas. There's often warm feeling towards others, particularly to those unemployed, homeless, old and alone.

7   Some teenagers hate Christmas Day. Boring. Want to be with friends rather than with family.

8   If it's a bore for you why not offer to help with a Christmas Day meal for old people or volunteer to help in a hospital or Children's Home? There are plenty of opportunities.

9   Christmas can be just eating, drinking and having a good time but is also celebration, for those who believe it, of one of the greatest events in history.

10   Charles Wesley, the hymn writer and brother of John Wesley, described this event as:

> 'God contracted to a span
> Incomprehensibly made man'.

11   Of course the question is: Is it true?

Listen to John Betjeman's poem 'Christmas'.

> The bells of waiting Advent ring,
>   The tortoise stove is lit again
> And lamp-oil light across the night
>   Has caught the streaks of winter rain
> In many a stained-glass window sheen
> From Crimson Lake to Hookers' Green.
>
> The holly in the windy hedge
>   and around the Manor House the yew
> Will soon be stripped to deck the ledge,
>   The altar, font and arch and pew
> So that the villagers can say
> 'The church looks nice' on Christmas Day.
>
> Provincial public houses blaze
>   And Corporation tramcars clang,
> On lighted tenements I gaze
>   Where paper decorations hang,
> And bunting in the red Town Hall
> Says 'Merry Christmas to you all.'
>
> And London shops on Christmas Eve
>   Are strung with silver bells and flowers

As hurrying clerks the city leave
   To pigeon-haunted classic towers,
And marbled clouds go scudding by
The many-steepled London sky.

And girls in slacks remember Dad
   And oafish louts remember Mum,
And sleepless children's hearts are glad,
   And Christmas-morning bells say 'Come!'
Even to shining ones who dwell
Safe in the Dorchester Hotel.

And is it true? And is it true,
   This most tremendous tale of all,
Seen in a stained-glass window's hue,
   A baby in an ox's stall?
The Maker of the stars and sea
Become a child on earth for me?

And is it true? For if it is,
   No loving fingers tying strings
Around those tissued fripperies,
   The sweet and silly Christmas things,
Bath salts and inexpensive scent
And hideous tie so kindly meant,

No love that in a family dwells,
   No carolling in frosty air,
Nor all the steeple-shaking bells
   Can with this single truth compare –
That God was man in Palestine
And lives today in Bread and Wine.

NOTES: CHRISTMAS

MIND OVER MATTER

1   Keeping body healthy very important.
Exercise and diet both crucial factors in bodily health.

2   EXERCISE: Unlike ancestors many people now sit at desk or ride in cars most of time.
             Chairs need to be carefully chosen.
             Important to sit properly on sitting-bones – not to slump.
             Great problems caused by slumping over desk.

             Cars one of biggest dangers to health
             Not just accidents but effect on back from sitting position.
             Also lack of exercise – e.g. jump in car just to go to corner shop.

3   Most important of all, however, is health of mind.

    Many people say; 'When I get old I hope I still have a healthy mind'.

4   Mind is more than brain.

    Mind governs whole being. Includes brain but represents:

             Drive, Energy, Will-power of our Personality.

5   Need to ensure minds are kept active; that we continue to find purpose and challenge in our lives.

6   It's mind that controls our well-being.
When depressed and low, doctors say, disease more easily attacks the body.
Mind is powerful influence over body.

7   Not just feeling better (which can be imaginary)
Mind actually helps to cure us.

    We can make our bodies healthier by thinking positively.

8   This has been proved by people who by strength of mind have defied doctor's diagnosis.

9   DANGER: Positive thinking does not always cure people. Some with strong positive thinking have bravely fought cancer, for example, and have still died.

10   Nevertheless, positive thinking always helps.
Negative thinking is destructive.

11   A healthy mind:

             Can keep us fit

Can make illness more bearable
And, in some cases, actually defeat a seemingly incurable disease.

12 Similarly attitude to disablement can make difference

(Interesting that some people choose to refer to the disabled as: Otherwise Enabled. It gives positive perspective rather than negative one).

PRAYER

In silence, if we are people who pray, let us pray for – if are not, then let us think about:

The importance of a healthy mind and the need to think positively;
Offering help, kindness and sympathy to those whose minds have broken down.

NOTES – MIND OVER MATTER

AGEISM

1 Prejudice comes in many forms.

   Sometimes subtle and unrecognised.
   Deeply rooted:
       Early years?
       Family?
       Friends?
       Media?
       Environment?

2 For example, Sexism and Racism.
   Issues confronted over last few decades.
   Still rife.

3 One prejudice not yet properly confronted: Ageism.
   People often very cruel about old people.

Use expressions like:
> 'Old Codger
> 'Silly Old Moo'.

(Expect laughter and think about how to react).

4. Organisations like Age Concern campaigning against Ageism.
E.g. Poster: 'How long before people start calling you names?'

5. When people are younger can be regarded as:
> Good looking
> Bright
> Interesting
> Important
> Well off, etc.

6. Time comes when only one epithet used: OLD.
All treated same whatever intelligence or experience.

7. Nowadays age can hit people much earlier:

   e.g. Adverts which say: 'No one over 40 need apply'.
   About half adverts for jobs mention age: Upper limit often 35.
   Early retirement commonly at 50–55.

8. For some, e.g. Sportspeople and Rock Stars, careers can finish in 20s or 30s.

9. On other hand Judges go on to 80+. (Should they?)

10. Very term 'old' has negative connotations

    e.g. opposite of 'new'.

11. As people live longer and number of pensioners soars, need to replace 'old' with new terms:
> e.g. Third and Fourth Ages.

    Even term 'Senior Citizen' is unpopular with number of older people.

12. Attitude of young must change
Need to think of older people as individuals with personal talents and wealth of experience.

    In family, Grandparents often greatly loved and respected by children.

13. People of Third and Fourth Age are not relics or wrecks:

    e.g. Shakespeare's caricature of Seventh Age in 'As You Like It'.

    'Last scene of all . . .
    Is second childishness and mere oblivion,
    Sans teeth, sans eyes, sans taste, sans everything'.

14 Quite to the contrary, these people are valuable assets whose maturity and wisdom can enrich our society.

15 What can we do as a school?

What can you do as a young person
    to work with, and educate yourself about, people of Third and Fourth Age?

PRAYER

Help us to learn respect for those who have reached the maturity of advanced years.
Give us understanding and sympathy, particularly for older people who no longer have the full use of their faculties.

NOTES – AGEISM

SCIENCE AND RELIGION

1 Some regard science and religion as opposing views of universe and meaning of life.

Others see science and religion as complementary:
    science – physical
    religion – spiritual

2 Scientists base knowledge on laws and theories they deduce from physical universe around them.

3 Religious persons base knowledge on faith in God and own personal spiritual experience.

4 Scientists seek proof before acceptance: analysis, synthesis, 'boiling in a test tube'.

5 Religious beliefs cannot be tested in same scientific way.
They are of different dimension, defying laboratory analysis.

6 This poem sums it up:

EACH IN HIS OWN TONGUE
by W. H. Carruth.

>A fire-mist and a planet,
>   A crystal and a cell,
>A jelly-fish and a saurian,
>   And caves where the cave-men dwell;
>Then a sense of law and beauty,
>   And a face turned from the clod –
>Some call it evolution,
>   And others call it God.
>
>A haze on the far horizon,
>   The infinite, tender sky,
>The ripe, rich tint of the cornfields,
>   And the wild geese sailing high;
>And all over upland and lowland
>   The charm of the golden rod –
>Some of us call it Autumn,
>   And others call it God.
>
>Like tides on a crescent sea-beach,
>   When the moon is new and thin,
>Into our hearts high yearnings
>   Come welling and surging in –
>Come from the mystic ocean
>   Whose rim no foot has trod –
>Some of us call it Longing
>   And others call it God.
>
>A picket frozen on duty –
>   A mother starved for her brood –
>Socrates drinking on the hemlock,
>   And Jesus on the rood;
>And millions who, humble and nameless,
>   The straight, hard pathway plod –
>Some call it Consecration,
>   And others call it God.

7 This next poem is about lawyers but, of course, it is a rash generalisation. There are plenty of sensitive lawyers.

8 It could apply to anybody who is unaware of the beauty of ordinary things.

Even the most highly trained and learned people do not always appreciate simple facts about Nature and the human heart.

THE LAW THE LAWYERS KNOW ABOUT
by H.D.C. Pepler.

The law the lawyers know about
Is property and land;
But why the leaves are on the trees;
And why the winds disturb the seas,
Why honey is the food of bees,
Why horses have such tender knees,
Why winters come and rivers freeze,
Why Faith is more than what one sees
And Hope survives the worst disease,
And Charity is more than these,
They do not understand.

PRAYER

Let us always be sensitive to the wonders of life and Nature. Help us to understand that personal experience can be as valid as physical proof.

NOTES: SCIENCE AND RELIGION

PESACH – JEWISH PASSOVER

1. Greatest festival of Jewish Year. (Pronounced Paysak – the last sound as in loch) Lasts for eight days. Celebrated in Springtime.

2. Reminds Jewish people of how God told Moses to lead people of Israel out of Egypt into Promised Land.

3   This took place about 3000 years ago.
    Story told in O.T. (see Exodus chapter 12).

4   Feast is called 'Passover' because Angel of Death killed first-born in every Egyptian household
    BUT *passed over* houses of Hebrews.

5   The Torah (Mosaic Law) decreed story of deliverance from Pharaoh should be told each year to children.

    Festival based on book called 'Haggadah' (Hebrew 'to tell').
    Contains the story, songs and prayers.

6   Before feast, house must be thoroughly cleaned; candles lit; cup of wine for everybody plus one for any unexpected guest. Special dishes prepared on Seder Plate.

7   Special foods include:

    – Unleavened bread ie without yeast
        (Recalling bread made in haste before Exodus)
    – Parsley dipped in salt:
        (Recalling tears shed in Egypt)
    – Roasted lamb:
        (Recalling lamb sacrificed on night before Exodus)
    – A roasted egg:
        (For new life)
    – A bitter herb: e.g. horseradish:
        (Recalling bitterness of slavery)
    – Paste of fruits:
        (recalling sweetness of deliverance)

8   As part of Festival, youngest child in family asks four questions about reason for Festival. Father reads answers from Haggadah.

9   After meal there are special prayers.

    Hymns said at home and in synaguoge in thankfulness for deliverance from Egypt and for present blessings.

10 Psalms 113 and 114 read as part of ceremony.

    (Psalm 114 is good, short example to read)

PRAYER (Psalm 115)

To you alone, O Lord, and not to us, must glory be given because of your constant love and faithfulness.

NOTES – PESACH – JEWISH PASSOVER

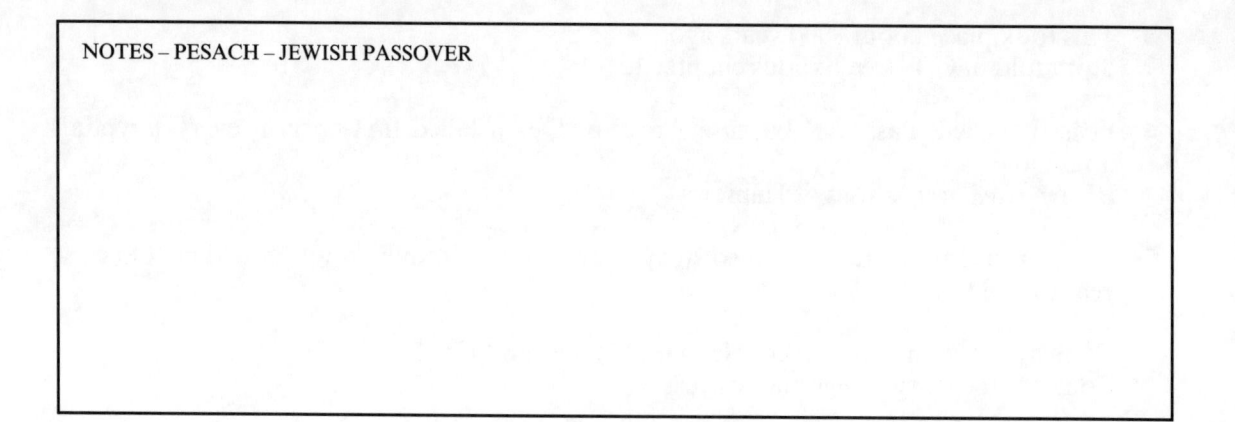

NATIONALISM

1. Most people proud of country of origin.
   (Not universally true. Some choose to leave; others forced to leave).

2. Group identity – Language, Customs, Food, etc.

3. In recent past nationalism been considered by many as divisive, unhelpful.

4. However, nationalism now on increase.
   Demand for separate states e.g. Russian States – Georgia, Armenia.

5. Even *within* states – e.g. former Yugoslavia, claims for division on ethnic lines.

6. Patriotism – love of country; representing country in sporting events, in one sense laudable; certainly understandable – Need of human beings to feel part of group (gregariousness). Sense of belonging e.g. club, team, uniforms.

7. BUT, inherent dangers in nationalism.

   REMINDER: Rise of Adolf Hitler, Leader of National-sozialisten Party (Nazis) in Germany in 1933.
   German leaders believed Nazis could not succeed as had only 3 out of 9 members in Cabinet.
   Chancellor at time (Franz Von Papen) stated:
       'We have Hitler boxed in'.
   Newspaper, Frankfurter Zeitung, reported:
       'The Nationalist Socialist attack has been repulsed'.
   'Nevertheless, Hitler appointed Chancellor'.
   Still not taken seriously abroad:
       France: Momentum of Nazis would recede.
       Britain: Hitler is 'man of straw'.
   History proved otherwise.

8 Question now is:

    Can National Socialism rise again?
    Some believe conditions similar to 1930s:
    – disillusion with mainstream politics
    – bitterness at state of economy
    – lethal attacks on foreigners.

9 Not confined to Germany:

    France – National Front
    Britain – British National Party.

10 Worse still: ethnic cleansing of minority groups in Europe and elsewhere.
Concentration camps, torture, rape, persecution.

11 Alarm bells beginning to ring.

    Delicate line between: pride of country
                             and hatred of foreigners.

12 In Britain mixture of races, creeds, colours and cultures.
Need for tolerance and understanding.

ABOVE ALL: Must educate children and young people in family and school to appreciate and learn to work alongside, and live in harmony with, people who are different from ourselves.

PRAYER

We believe, O God, that you regard all human beings as of equal value.
May we learn to judge people, not by their outward appearance but by their inner worth.

NOTES – NATIONALISM

EUTHANASIA

1. Dictionary definition:

    'Bringing about of gentle and easy death in case of incurable and painful disease'.

2. Newspaper headline:

    'Dr X will be sentenced today for attempted murder of one of his 70-year-old patients.'

3. Extremely controversial issue.

    AGAINST: Involves religious, ethical and moral principles:
    – human life is sacred. No-one has right to terminate it.
    – miracles can happen. Person could suddenly recover.
    – opens door to abuse. Relatives and doctors could dispatch unwanted, troublesome patients.

    FOR: It's the only humane way of dealing with it:
    – people should have right to choose time of death
    – why should people have to endure excruciating pain?
    – we don't let pets suffer. Put down without questions.
    – death should be dignified.

4. Terence Higgins Trust and Centre of Medical Law and Ethics at King's College, London have drawn up document – 'Living Will'.
    Designed for people with HIV and AIDS.
    (Terence Higgins Trust is counselling service for HIV and AIDS)
    But document can be used by anybody worried about situation at end of life.

5. Most fully researched and complete document of its kind.
    Addresses three possible health conditions:
    – terminal stages of incurable physical illness
    – permanent mental impairment and incurable physical illness
    – permanent unconsciousness.

6. People can choose:
    – to be kept alive as long as possible
    – not to be kept alive
    – to have treatment for pain relief only.

7. Additional clauses enable patient to:
    – appoint health care proxy
    – take part in medical decisions
    – be kept alive so that named person can see them before they die.

8   No law in UK specifically dealing with 'Living Wills'.
    Common, however, in USA.
    English Court of Appeal has:
    > 'strongly indicated that a properly prepared 'Living Will' would be binding on doctors'.

9   There may be still some way to go before any such procedures would be fully legal.

10 Obviously significant number of people may still have serious and valid objections to any form of euthanasia.

11 What do you think?

    Would any students be prepared to take further assembly on this issue, presenting both sides?

NOTES – EUTHANASIA

IN THE BEGINNING

1   How did it all begin? Where does the Universe come from?

2   Famous conundrum –

    Which came first – chicken or egg?

    The egg which produced chicken? Where did egg come from?
    The chicken which produced egg? Where did chicken come from?

3   No simple answer.

    We do know chickens evolved, as we have, from more primitive forms of life.

4   Solar system goes back thousands of millions of years:

- Began with finely dispersed dust and gas rotating; concentrating gradually under gravitational forces.
- Heat of process produced dimly glowing infant sun with flat disc of gas around it.
- Within disc gas condensed to form earth and other planets.

5
4700 million years ago
Earth cooled. Gases became liquid. Solid particles of crust appeared.

3000 million years ago
Complex soup of chemicals essential to life formed.
Produced molecules. From combination of molecules came living cells.

1500 million years ago
Habitable planet

1200 million years ago
Organisms with more than one cell

450 million years ago
Sea plants got grip on dry land

380 million years ago
Animals invaded land, led by amphibians.

325 million years ago
Amphibians followed by reptiles.
Recognisable insects appeared.

150 million years ago
Sky filled with pterodactyls.
(On land dinosaurs etc)

70 million years ago
Dinosaurs disappeared

40 million years ago
Species of primates – common ancestors of great apes and humans.

20 million years ago
Some began to walk upright.

5 million years
Earliest trace of human-like creatures in Africa.
(Africa generally assumed cradle of mankind).

10,000 years ago
Far more advanced human – Homo Sapiens.
Distinguished by use of tools.

(CAUTION: Theories may need updating).

6 Bible says:
'In the beginning God made the heavens and the earth'

7 Two views not necessarily contradictory.

Natural History Museum in London now portrays both views.

8 Whether start with evolution or God, still left with question:

> How did it all begin? (Back to chicken and egg!)
> What did it all evolve from?

9 Scientists say: Matter cannot be created or destroyed.
    If so, matter has always existed.

10 BUT what does 'Always' mean?
    'For ever'?
We humans can't understand that.
For us everything has beginning and end.
One of our favourite questions is: 'When did it start?'
Another is: 'When is it going to finish?'

11 If you divide 10 by 3 = 3.333+.
In other words goes on to infinity.

Space also apparently never finishes.

12 What do such things mean?

Maybe higher intelligences exist who understand but human brain limited.

13 Left with two viable options:

   1) God (being not limited by physical laws) created 'heavens and earth'.
   2) 'Big Bang Theory' – Explosion in which gases thrown out, solidified and our universe evolved.
      (Or an alternative theory to this one).

14 Question still remains: Where did it all come from?

   (a) Those who do not accept concept of God either accept they do not know or believe one day answer will be found.
   (b) Those who believe in God say He is Spiritual Being who has existed for ever and at beginning of Time created basis from which all has evolved. In other words everything came from God.

   John Dryden (1631–1700) sums up theist's position succinctly at end of poem: 'Reason and Religion'.

   'How can the less the greater comprehend?
   Or finite reason reach Infinity?
   For what could fathom God were more than he.'

NOTES – IN THE BEGINNING

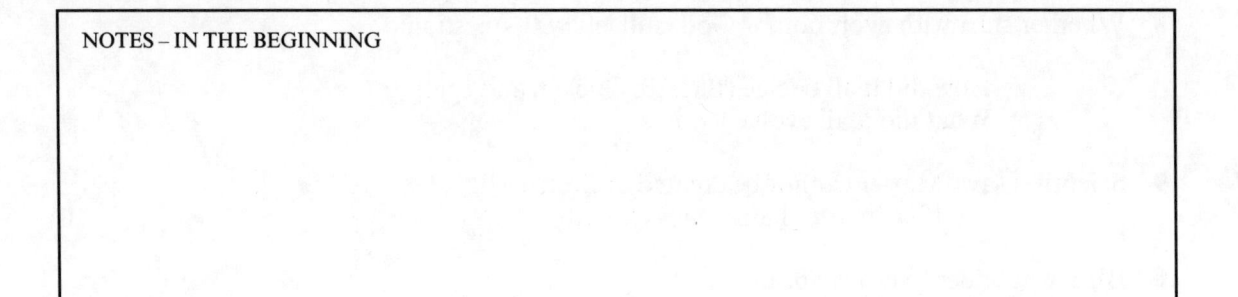

SLAVERY

1 SONG:
>'John Brown's body lies a'mouldring in the grave,
>But his soul goes marching on.'

   (Once a popular community song. Is it still known?)

2 People who sang/sing it probably didn't/don't know who or what it is about.

3 John Brown born in USA in 1800.
   Campaigned for abolition of slavery.
   Many slaves at that time in southern States of America.
   New ones still being brought over from Africa.

4 Attempts to free slaves by peaceful means had failed.
   JB decided violence was only answer.
   Freed some slaves from owners and helped them to escape to Canada.

5 Then JB organised slave revolt. Needed weapons so overpowered guards at arsenal at Harper's Ferry, Virginia and stole guns. Trapped in building by local people, taken prisoner and put on trial.

6 JB found guilty of murder and treason.
   Hanged on 2 Dec. 1859.

7 Unfortunately, JB's efforts only increased dissension about slavery.
   But for pro-freedom lobby became martyr.
   Hence marching song composed in his honour.

8 Year later (1860), Abraham Lincoln became President of USA.
   Believed strongly in freedom for slaves.
   Civil war broke out between North and South USA over issue of slavery, (North-against; South-for).

9 January 1863 Emancipation Proclamation made. (Law freeing all slaves throughout USA.)

10   Lincoln assassinated in 1863.

      Nevertheless, in 1865 Civil Rights Act passed.
      Guaranteed rights of all US citizens – black and white.

11   Issue had still to be pursued in USA.

        e.g. campaigning of Martin Luther King contributed to
             passing of Civil Rights Act (1964)
             and Voting Rights Act (1965).

12   King too was assassinated in Memphis, Tennessee, 4 April 1968.

13   In this country, William Wilberforce led Parliamentary campaign to abolish slave trade. (Achieved in 1807).

      Slavery in British Empire abolished in 1833.

14   Is slavery abolished?

      Officially. But many people, including children, in many countries still enslaved.
      Even in this country reports of foreign servants brought in and made to work like slaves.

15   We must not rest until *all* are treated equally regardless of colour, creed, race or gender.

THOUGHT FOR DAY:

When Jesus began public ministry he set out his manifesto. Let's listen to his words:
(Good News Bible version)

> 'The Spirit of the Lord is upon me,
>   because he has chosen me to bring
>   good news to the poor.
> He has sent me to proclaim liberty to
>   the captives
> and recovery of sight to the blind;
> to set free the oppressed
> and announce that the time has come
> when the Lord will save his people'.

NOTES – SLAVERY

MURDER

1. Most older people, when asked, know where they were when President John F. Kennedy was assassinated. (Dallas 22 Nov 1963).

2. Similarly, older teenagers may remember when John Lennon was assassinated, (1980).

3. Shock to all lovers of Beatles. Senseless, mad.

4. In Sunday paper in Jan. 1981 whole page taken up with letter from Yoko Ono, Lennon's wife.

    Entitled: 'In Gratitude'. Yoko said:

    > 'I am angry at myself and all of us for allowing our society to fall apart to this extent. The only revenge that would mean anything to us is to turn the society around in time to one that is based on love and trust as John felt it could be. The only solace is to show that it could be done, that we could create a world of peace on earth for each other and for our children.'

5. Was terrible event but is one of thousands of such murders.
   Some, like John's, seem senseless and motiveless.
   Others are for sex, money, drugs or revenge.

6. Yoko says:

    > 'allowing our society to fall apart'.

    Sadly, it has always been pretty much like that. In fact, in past e.g. Roman era, Middle Ages, torture, pillage, rape, murder were much worse.

7. There is difference:

    THEN: it was taken for granted;
    NOW: we believe we know better. Don't take it for granted.

8. Cruel fact is: we may *know* better but we don't *do* any better.

9. People will continue to use violence, cruelty, murder as long as it serves selfish purpose.

10. Yoko went on to give her answer to the problem:

    > 'If all of us just loved and cared for one person each. That is all it takes. Love breeds love. Maybe then, we will be able to prevent each other from going insane. Maybe then, we will be able to prevent each other from becoming violent, as violence is in our hearts and not in weapons. Guilt is not in the one who pulls the trigger but in each of us who allows it.'

11 (Optional ending) Play tape/disc/record of:
　　'All you need is Love' – by John Lennon.

NOTES – MURDER

RELIGIONS

1 Religion important part of human life.

　Goes right back to beginnings of human history.
　Every tribe had religious belief independently. Not copied.

2 Explanation?

　Is it conditioning – Passed on?
　Is it born in us – Part of our human nature to believe in supernatural?

3 Vast variety of religions:

　　Major: (Alphabetically) Buddhism, Christianity, Hinduism, Islam, Judaism, Sikhism.

　　Less well known:　Shintoism (ancient religion of Japan)
　　　　　　　　　　Confucianism and Taoism (religions of China).
　　　　　　　　　　Baha'i (originated in Persia).
　　　　　　　　　　Zoroastrianism (ancient religion of Persia).
　　　　　　　　　　Jainism (mainly in Gujarat and Mysore in India).

4 People mostly belong to religion of family/country in which born.

　Exceptions: some converted from one religion to another.

5 Obviously, whatever religion you belong to, believe it's best, has greatest truth.

　Trouble is people go further and believe all others are wrong.
　Led to wars and bloodshed, e.g. The Crusades.

6   Even today great religions conflict:

>   Jew v Arab,
>   Christian v Muslim
>   Hindu v Sikh

    and vice-versa.

7   Some religions claim they have never shed drop of human blood for their religion (e.g. Buddhist) but most would rather die than see their religion destroyed.

8   Few parts of world free from religious rivalry and intolerance.
    (e.g. former Yugoslavia).
    Exists even *within* Christian Church (e.g. N. Ireland).

9   Part of our job in school is to promote religious tolerance:

    – live and let live
    – respect one another's beliefs
    – allow others to worship in peace in own way.

    (If part of school aims quote relevant section/s).

10 You are growing up in multi-faith society.
    So many people of different persuasions live side by side

11 What can we do?

    One important thing is to learn all we can about other religions.

    Ignorance breeds misunderstanding and even hatred.
    Quite horrifying the myths that exist about what other religions believe and do.

12 (Optional)
    In next few weeks I shall invite students/local reps. of different faiths to give us short insight into their religion.

PRAYER

Whatever our own personal beliefs, teach us to be tolerant, respecting the freedom of others to believe and worship in accordance with their convictions.

NOTES – RELIGIONS

POVERTY

1. What is definition of poverty?

    Two approaches:
    (a) *Resources for Subsistence*: B. S. Rowntree in 'Poverty and Progress: A Second Social Survey of York (1941) defines Poverty Line as:
    "the minimum from which physical efficiency could be maintained. A bare standard of subsistence rather than living."
    (b) *Citizenship Standard*: People who lack resources required to participate in life of community.

2. Survey from London Weekend Television found most people agreed following was minimum necessary for participation in society:

    - self-contained damp-free accommodation with indoor toilet and bath.
    - weekly roast joint for family and three daily meals for each child.
    - two pairs of all-weather shoes and warm waterproof coat
    - sufficient money for public transport
    - adequate bedrooms and beds
    - refrigerator and washing machine
    - enough money for special occasions like Christmas
    - toys for children.

    (Above might be better displayed on flip-chart or OHP).

3. Published low income figures for Britain in 1987:
    - 10 million living in poverty or below subsistence level, including 3 million children

    (15 million, if we accept Citizenship Standard as marker, = 1/4 of population)

4. What about attitudes to poverty?

    Varying views:
    - it does not exist
    - poor should get off bottoms and do something for themselves
    - why should these people have washing-machine or refrigerator?
    - it is most scandalous feature of our society.

5. Contributing factors:

    - unemployment (dramatically increased)
    - low pay (especially for women)
    - disability
    - inadequate State pensions and child benefits.

6. Overall contributing factor is deficiencies in social policies. Hard truth is our economic, social and political institutions operate to produce both wealth and poverty.

7   What do you think?
    Are there other explanations for causes of poverty?
    What are solutions?
    Are we who are comfortably off responsible for less fortunate?
    Should rich be made to pay for poor?

    (Students could be invited to put their views to next assembly).

```
NOTES – POVERTY



```

REFUGEES

(Select material or spread over two assemblies).

1   Every day heartrending stories of refugees fleeing country.
            (Use topical examples).

2   What is definition of *refugee*?

    What about those leaving Eastern Europe in 1989?
    Or Vietnamese boat people in Hong Kong camps?

3   UN 1951 Convention relating to The Status of Refugees (and associated Protocol of 1967), defines refugee as:

    'person who, owing to a well-founded fear of being persecuted for reasons of race, religion, nationality, membership in a particular social group or political opinion, is outside the country of his/her nationality and does not have the protection of a national government.'

4   People migrating simply to find employment or better standard of living are 'economic migrants'
            (Polite term for 'illegal immigrants').

5   Reasons for people seeking refuge:
        – war and civil unrest
        – persecution
        – environmental disaster (e.g. global warming)
        – degradation of agricultural land (e.g. becoming desert).

6 At end of 1991, estimated 17 million refugees fled home countries.

   Millions more displaced within national borders.
   Altogether this represents about 30 million people.

7 Situation of refugees one of earliest concerns of UN. Article 14 of Universal Declaration of Human Rights (1948) states:

   'Everyone has the right to seek and enjoy in other countries asylum from persecution.'

8 1946 UN established International Refugee Organisation (IRO).
   1951 Became clear IRO would not solve whole refugee problem.
       UN created Office of High Commissioner for Refugees (UNHCR)
       Since established, UNHCR has helped some 26 million refugees to find durable solutions to problems.

9 UNHCR offers:

   – international protection (asylum and favourable legal status)
   – material assistance (food, shelter, medical aid)
   – voluntary repatriation
   – local integration (to become self-supporting)
   – resettlement (in countries other than one that gave shelter)

10 Staff of about 2000 work at UNHCR in Geneva and 100 other countries.
   Total cost of activities in 1991: over 850 million US dollars.

11 Problems increasing. Growing reluctance of countries to accept refugees:

   – fear of mass migration
   – group refugees with terrorists and drug-runners
   – considered security risk
   – problems of finding employment.

12 EC governments making borders more difficult to penetrate.
   UK Home Secretary in July 1991 announced tighter controls on asylum seekers.

13 What do asylum seekers need to get fair deal?

   – reception arrangements which ease arrival
   – sympathetic interpreters
   – temporary accommodation
   – well trained, sensitive immigration officials
   – access to legal aid.

14 UN has said:

   'The political and economic turmoil of our time can be traced in the footsteps of people on the move'.

15 Followed by 'Discuss', would make good 'A' Level question!
    (Certainly something senior students might like to discuss).

16 Plight of refugees now universal problem.

    Persecution and 'ethnic cleansing'* on increase.
    Refugees scattered in virtually every continent.

    (*May need simple explanation)

17 Major governments must co-operate in finding solutions

    BUT, in final analysis, according to UN, country of origin must accept responsibility for own citizens both in terms of preventing situations which can give rise to refugee flows and creating conditions which allow safe and voluntary return.

    PRAYER:

    In silence, let us remember the plight of those who have, for whatever reason, have been made to leave their country of origin, thanking God for the security we enjoy.

NOTES – REFUGEES.

HANDEL'S MESSIAH – CHRISTMAS

(This assembly could be used other than at Christmas
if material specific to Christmas is omitted).

1 Christmas celebration of Christ's birth.

   Music plays great part in celebrations.
   Began with chorus of angels in Bible story who sang:
        'Glory to God in the highest
        Peace on earth and goodwill to all people'.

2 Hebrew for Christ is 'Messiah'.

Many quotations used at Christmas time as part of religious celebrations, e.g. Nine Lessons and Carols, which are prophecies about the Messiah, come from Old Testament, (e.g. Isaiah).

3. Christians believe Jesus was long expected Messiah.
   Theme of his birth, life and death have inspired many musicians,
         e.g. Bach, Mozart, Verdi, etc. (add names as you wish).

4. Handel wrote oratorio entitled: 'The Messiah'.
   Performed at numerous venues every Christmas and Easter.

5. George Frederic Handel born in Halle in Germany in 1685 (same year as Bach)
   Became internationally famous during tour of Italy (1706–1709).
   Wrote operas, oratorios and church and chamber music.
   Settled in England in 1712.
   Among other things wrote Ode for Queen's Birthday (1713) and Water Music (1717).
   From 1720, as Director of Royal Academy of Music, composed more than 30 Italian operas including Julius Caesar (1724), and Xerxes, (1738) (containing famous Largo).
   Italian opera lost popularity, so turned to oratorios
   e.g. Judas Maccabaeus (1747) and most well-known of all, The Messiah. (1742)

6. The Messiah – oratorio for solo voices, choir and orchestra to text arranged from Bible by Charles Jenner.
   Three Parts tell events of Jesus's life and death.
   Several individual pieces famous in own right;
         e.g. Hallelujah Chorus.

7. Handel wrote Messiah in three weeks.
   Some critics say would have been better if taken longer!

8. Let's finish by listening to Chorus that specifically refers to birth of Jesus: 'Unto us a Child is Born'.
         ('Glory to God in the Highest' may be preferred.)

NOTES – HANDEL'S MESSIAH

SHINTOISM

1. Buddhism said to have meant more to Japan than to China.

Developed several new schools of thought.

(Zen, Shingon, Tendai).

2 Confucianism refined Japanese civilisation.

Confucius (551-479BC). Self-educated.
Provided blueprint for behaviour of individuals, society and governments.

3 BUT Japan's own native religious product is Shintoism.
Essentially tribal religion.

4 Embraces cults of Nature in its varied manifestations.

5 Abundance of myths surround these cults. Concerned with essential unity of life, and Nature as true object of worship.

6 To Japanese does not matter whether one god or many, because really worshipping, in many forms, the one ever-present and ever-active life manifest equally in Nature, men and gods.

7 BUT, in worshipping, Japanese focus all on national life.
Head and guardian of all cults is Emperor descended from Sun-goddess, Amaterasu.

8 Important Japanese festival is Hollyhock Festival.
Held in Kyoto, old capital of Japan.
On 15th May, hollyhocks offered to gods at Shinto shrines.
First held about thousand years ago.
Flowers offered to appease gods when crops devastated by weather.

9 Another Japanese flower festival is Cherry Blossom Festival.
Held in Spring. Special dances performed in theatres in Kyoto and Tokyo.

10 Certain rituals (particularly June and December) observed in Shinto temples.
Designed to drive away evil and impurities.

11 Ganjitsu (New Year) is most important Japanese holiday.
Lasts 6 days. Time of family reunions.
Sometimes piece of soil containing family god sent to those unable to return home.

12 On eve of New Year 108 peals of bells ring at Shinto shrines to show evil been removed.

NOTES – SHINTOISM

HOLY WEEK
ART AND RELIGION

1. Painting and religion always had close relationship:

    – both make ordinary appear extraordinary
    – both add touch of mystery to everyday.

2. Visit any major art gallery in Western world.
   Will find sizeable proportion of paintings with religious themes.

3. In particular, life, death and Resurrection of Jesus has inspired many famous artists.

   Some suggest parallel between miracles of Christianity and miracle of art.

4. (Photocopy picture by William Holman Hunt: *'The Shadow of Death'* at *back of book on page* 127. Either distribute copies to assembly or use OHP.)

   William Holman Hunt, Dante Gabriel Rossetti and John Everett Millais together founded Pre-Raphaelite Brotherhood in 1848.
   Considered most influential movement in history of English art.
   Influence on art and literature lasted through 19th century and into 20th century.

5. Brotherhood was secret society like other revolutionary groups of time. Called themselves Pre-Raphaelites.

   Reflected admiration for early Italian painters before Raphael.
   Wanted to:
    – emulate honesty and simplicity of these early Christian painters
    – paint nobler, more serious pictures such as 'turned the minds of men to good reflections'.

6. Condemned prevailing tide of triviality and vulgarity in art.

   Determined to:
    – be completely faithful to nature
    – study each figure from a model
    – paint landscapes on the spot, out-of-doors.

   Used pure colours over white background, making pictures appear startlingly bright.

7. 'The Shadow of the Cross' painted by Holman Hunt in a carpenter's shop in Bethlehem.
   Took immense pains to get every detail of workshop and tools correct.
   Later continued painting picture on Jerusalem rooftop, ensuring effect of full sunlight.
   Christ, stretching himself after labouring in workshop, unwittingly predicts crucifixion which mother sees on wall.

8 At end of week/next week is, Good Friday, when we remember crucifixion of Jesus.

9 Jesus, as in picture, foresaw own death.
Claimed to be Son of God and able to forgive sins.
Jews regarded this as blasphemy and sent him to Roman Procurator, Pontius Pilate, to be tried.
Pilate reluctantly sentenced him to death by crucifixion.
Often regarded as one of most painful forms of execution.

10 Christians believe Jesus:

- rose from dead
- is alive today
- offers eternal life to those who believe in him.

MEDITATION
(Poem by Helen Poore, 10 years)

Guardian of peace, shadowed on a cross to die.
Light feareth the cursed night.
A set picture of fear, engraved in the dark sky.
Bells ring his death . . .

But he shall rise, rise to the paradise,
Rise into freedom.

NOTES – HOLY WEEK ART AND RELIGION

THE FUTURE – WHAT DOES IT HOLD

1 People have always tried to look into future.

Fascinated by it.
Popular magazines and newspapers claim readers demand horoscopes.

2   Most of us read 'our stars' at some time or other.

   Either take it very seriously or treat it as bit of fun.
   Even for sceptics, suspicion at back of mind there's some truth in it.

3   However, most horoscopes seem very ambiguous – even amusing.

   e.g. You could come into some money but be careful who you trust.

   13th could be unlucky for you. 26th could be your special day but don't expect too much!

4   Some people try to predict their future with ouija boards.

   (Explain – usually round table with letters arranged round outside. All sit in silence, with eyes closed waiting for message supposedly from spirit world. Person receiving message guided to move finger to letters spelling out message).

5   Whether true or not, can be quite frightening:

   e.g. case of woman whose death was predicted by board for following February, died in that month.

   Prediction? Auto-suggestion? Who knows?

6   In book called 'Walk-About' by J.B. Marshall:

   Australian Aborigine on Walk-About (to prove his manhood) meets two Americans whose plane has crashed.
   Aborigine helps them in many ways, but woman brought up with prejudice against blacks and is frightened of his blackness and nakedness.
   Shows fear. Aborigine believes she shows fear because she can see his death.
   Aborigine catches cold, lies down and dies.

7   Witch doctors known to have had similar effect.

8   Don't know future. Most people glad.

   Do we really want to know what is going to happen?
   Could be wonderful; could be terrible.

9   Fatalists believe we have no influence over our future.

   Fate decides. Future inevitable.
   Recurring theme of many of great tragedies,
       e.g. ('King Lear')
           'As flies to wanton boys are we to the gods,
           They kill us for their sport.'

('Hamlet'):
'There's a divinity that shapes our ends,
Rough-hew them how we will.'

10. Conversely, some believe future is matter of chance.
Cannot be predicted. Could develop thousand different ways.

11. Christians take middle line.

    God guides us but we have freedom to choose whether to accept that guidance.
    According to decisions we make, so we carve out our future.
    Need to tune in to God's wavelength so that we can find his will for us.

12. Jesus often misquoted as having said:

    'Take no thought for the morrow'.
    Newer versions correctly translate this as:
    'Be not **anxious** about tomorrow'
    which is quite different!

13. All need to make suitable and sensible provision for future.
    What we must avoid at all costs is worry and anxiety about it.

    PRAYER

    Help us to avoid anxiety and stress in our lives.
    Teach us to live each day fully as it comes whilst at the same time paying due regard to the future.

NOTES – THE FUTURE

DESPAIR

1. Black moments in everybody's life.
   Times of depression, loneliness, despair.

2. Something we need to recognise and try to understand.

Helps to make us realise it is quite common.
If you feel desperate, then know many others have been there too.

YOU ARE NOT A FREAK.

3. Such feelings, or mood, can, however be very unnerving, disturbing.
   Some contemplate suicide.
   Some actually commit suicide.

4. Been suggested perhaps some young people who commit suicide have not really understood finality of death.
   Can't be just a gesture. No coming back.

5. Seems to be an answer: thought of peace, no worries,

   BUT eliminates possibility of fulfilling oneself in this life.

6. Life today very complex, stressful, confusing.
   Many young people feel there's no real future: for them, country, world.

   What's the use? Why bother?
   What's the point of living?

7. Poet, John Clare, (1793-1864), self-educated son of farm labourer in Northamptonshire, after achieving fame with first book: 'Poems Descriptive of Rural Life and Scenery', was less successful with three further volumes, including best-known work, 'The Shepherd's Calendar', and lived in great poverty. In 1837 became insane and was confined to lunatic asylum, where wrote some of best poems.

8. In this poem expresses his feeling of isolation and total disillusionment with everything. His deepest wish is to 'opt out', be released, return to simplicity and innocence of childhood.

I AM

I AM: yet what I am none cares or knows,
    My friends forsake me like a memory lost;
I am the self-consumer of my woes,
    They rise and vanish in oblivious host,
Like shades in love and death's oblivion lost;
And yet I am, and live with shadows tost.
Into the nothingness of scorn and noise,
    Into the living sea of waking dreams,
Where there is neither sense of life nor joys,
    But the vast shipwreck of my life's esteems;
And e'en the dearest – that I loved the best –
    Are strange – nay, rather stranger than the rest.

> I long for scenes where man has never trod,
>   A place where woman never smiled or wept;
> There to abide with my Creator, God,
>   And sleep as I in childhood sweetly slept:
> Untroubling and untroubled where I lie,
>   The grass below – above the vaulted sky.

9 When feeling rejected and alone natural to look back to happier times and wish once again we were able to sleep

> 'as I in childhood sweetly slept'.

10 That's why increasingly people now look to therapy.
Offers many with deep-seated psychological difficulties, often traceable to experiences of childhood.

11 What we all need is help to understand our inner selves.

We need someone to talk to.
Trained listeners; not to provide answers, but, give time and space and confidence from neutral position to think through our complex thoughts and emotions.

12 If you feel alone and rejected, find someone to talk to.

There are trained listeners here in school (School Counsellor?)
Life is never as bad as it appears in our blackest moments.

13 For some, religion is an answer:

> faith in God
> prayer
> meeting for worship and study
> confiding in priest/vicar/minister.

14 All you have to do is say 'Help' and you will find ready listeners.

FINAL THOUGHT

> Somewhere in this
> hopeless whirlpool of life–
> a hand extends to help.
>   (Woon Lai Eng, Singapore)

NOTES – DESPAIR

A reproduction of Holman Hunt's
'THE SHADOW OF THE CROSS'

INDEX

Advice 38
Ageism 98
Amnesty International 67
Apartheid 36
April 66
Art, and Religion 121
Attention to Detail 73
Bannister, Roger 84
Baptism 35
Benenson, Peter 68
Blindness 59
Blue Cross 9
Books 93
Booth, Rev. William 27
Brown, John 110
Buddhism 13, 119
Cadbury Bros 56
Chinese Festivals 41
Christmas 4, 94
    Decorations and
        Preparations 29
    Handel's Messiah 118
Clare, John 125
Community Responsibility 64
Compliments 15
Concentration 52
Confidence, Keeping a 14
Confucius 120
Conscientious Objectors 70
Counselling 38, 125
Dancing 71
Death (member of school) 79
Despair 124
Determination 83
Easter Sunday 34
End of School Year 23
End of Term 17
Environment 90
Euthanasia 106
Fishing (Sea) 77
Flowers 48
Friendship 85
Future 122
George, St 66
Giving 12
Gobind Singh, Guru 19, 66
Good Friday 33, 121
Guru Granth Sahib 19
Handel, George Frederic 119
Haves/Havenots 57

Health (Mind and Body) 97
Help 38
Hinduism: Holi 39
Holidays 18, 23
Holy Spirit 35
Holy Week 121
Home 10
Honesty 43
Hospitals 5
Huddleston, Father Trevor 36
Hunger 40
Hunt, William Holman 121
Ikebana 48
Islam 13, 22
Jewish Passover 102
Judaism 13
Kennedy, John F. 111
King, Martin Luther 111
Kipling, Rudyard 16, 86
Leavers' Assembly 25
Lennon, John 111
Lincoln, Abraham 110
Loyala, St Ignatius 13
Malnutrition 40
Maundy Thursday 31
Messiah (Handel) 118
Millais, John Everett 121
Mind, the 97
Mohammed, Prophet 22
Morality 82
Mothering Sunday 50
Murder 112
Muslim Calendar 22
Nanak, Guru 19
National Children's Home 54
Nationalism 104
Nature 101, 120
Nutrition 40
Ono, Yoko 111
Pacifism 69
Parables 57
Parents 7
Patience 76
PDSA 9
Peace-keeping 69
Peacemaking 36
Pentecost 35
Pesach 102
Pets 9
Poverty 115

Pre-Raphaelites 121
Qur'an 22
Rahere (Court Jester) 5
Reading 93
Red Indians 7
Refugees 116
Reliability 11
Religion 113
    and Art 121
    and Science 100
Remembrance Day 15
Rest 18, 23
Rossetti, Dante Gabriel 121
Royal British Legion 16
Royal National Institute for
    the Blind 60
Royal National Lifeboat
    Institution 78
RSPCA 9
Salvation Army 27
Science 100
Self-improvement 61
Selflessness 26
Shakespeare, William 67
Shintoism 119
Sikhism 6
    Guru Tegh Bahadur 6
Sincerity 75
Slavery 110
Spring 48
Sword of Damocles 49
Talents 63
Tegh Bahadur, Guru 6
Television 93
Thankfulness 44
Tongue, Controlling 14
Town Planning 55
Tutu, Archbishop Desmond 36
Unemployment 26, 28
UNHCR 117
United Nations 69, 116
Universe, Beginning of 107
Vanity 88
Violence 91
War 15, 69
Water 46
Whitsun 35
Wilberforce, William 110
Work 28
World Problems 20